Thomas Carly
The French

Dr Ruth Scurr is Fellow and Director of Studies in Politics at Gonville and Caius College, Cambridge. Her first book *Fatal Purity: Robespierre and the French Revolution* was published by Chatto and Windus in 2006 and was included in The 100 Best Books of the Decade by *The Times* in 2009. Dr Scurr writes regularly in the UK for *The Times, Times Literary Supplement* and the *Telegraph*, and for *The Nation* in the USA.

CONTINUUM HISTORIES
The greatest narrative history writing in English

This series is designed to attract a new generation of readers to some of the greatest narrative history ever written. Each volume includes a dramatic episode from a major work of history, prefaced with an introduction by a leading modern authority.

Continuum Histories demonstrate the extraordinary tradition that exists of great history writing in the English language – and that often the best stories are true stories.

Series Editor: Mark Bostridge

The French
Revolution

Also in Continuum Histories

William H. Prescott's *History of the Conquest of Mexico*.
Introduced and selected by J.H. Elliott

J.A. Froude's *The Reign of Mary Tudor*.
Introduced and selected by Eamon Duffy

Lord Macaulay's *History of England*.
Introduced and selected by John Burrow

Edward Gibbon's *Decline and Fall of the Roman Empire*.
Introduced and selected by Tom Holland (forthcoming)

Thomas Carlyle

The French
Revolution

Introduced and selected by
Ruth Scurr

continuum

Published by the Continuum International Publishing Group

The Tower Building	80 Maiden Lane
11 York Road	Suite 704
London	New York
SE1 7NX	NY 10038

www.continuumbooks.com

First published 2010

British Library Cataloguing-in-Publication Data
A catalogue record for this book is available from the British Library.

ISBN 978-0826-44052-5

Designed and typeset by www.benstudios.co.uk
Printed and bound by MPG Books Group Ltd

CONTENTS

INTRODUCTION

'Do you not know the Scottish word threep?' Thomas Carlyle asked his friend John Sterling on 17 January 1837, five days after finishing the third and final volume of *The French Revolution: A History*. 'I had taken a threep that I would write to no one, that I would not quit London, or know any rest satisfaction or pleasure of life till the despicability of a task were done.'[1] London at that time was bitterly cold, everything, even clothing, was frozen when he woke in the mornings, but Carlyle's obstinate decision had not been in vain. As he wrote to Sterling from his rented house in Cheyne Row, Chelsea, his manuscript was at the printer's; and he hoped it would only be a matter of weeks until he could wash his hands of it for 'forever and a day'. The book had absorbed his energies since 1834:

> It is a wild savage Book, itself a kind of French Revolution;—which perhaps, if Providence have so ordered it, the world had better *not* accept when offered it? With all my heart! What I do know of it is that it has come hot out of my own soul; born in blackness whirlwind and sorrow; that no man, for a long while, has stood speaking so completely alone

under the Eternal Azure, in the character of man only; or is likely for a long while so to stand:—finally that it has gone as near to choking the life out of me as any task I should like to undertake for some years to come; which also is an immense comfort, indeed the greatest of all.[2]

The term exhaustion scarcely covered the state he was in: he wanted to weep and pray when he put down his pen, but did not do either 'at least not visibly or audibly.'[3] He was poor, he had a sick wife to support and his own health was fragile. He was 42 and had long hoped to live by writing, but his only substantial work so far, *Sartor Resartus*, (an experimental narrative serialized in *Fraser's Magazine* in 1833–4) had met with general bafflement.[4] For his book on the French Revolution, Carlyle had a 'half-profits' contract with his publisher, James Fraser, which would give him no income from the finished text until the production and printing costs had been recouped.[5] Only then would he be entitled to half of any money it might make. Even though he was due to publish essays on The Diamond Necklace Affair and Mirabeau in 1837, alongside his monumental history of the Revolution, for the foreseeable future Carlyle was going to have to lecture for an income.

In the circumstances, to flirt with the idea of the world not accepting the book to which he had given so much of himself, and on which so much of his economic future rode was somewhat perverse; yet it fitted with Carlyle's and posterity's understanding of the prophetic (or preternatural) nature of his text. Alone, under an eternal sky, speaking in the voice of mankind, Carlyle had all but reenacted the French

Revolution for himself and his readers. He had got as close to the chaos and violence as he could, and let it speak through his incendiary style, rolling from one dramatic episode to the next, with no respite and scarcely even pause for breath. No wonder he could not stop, was taking threeps to keep distraction at bay until his narrative, like the Revolution itself, ended abruptly with the death of Robespierre.

The sensation of being dragged along, faster and faster, through unstoppably darkening events is familiar to all who work on the Revolution, and resonates with the memoirs of its survivors. Carlyle was the first historian to capture that trajectory of frightening acceleration into Bedlam: the first to locate it at the heart of his narrative. His initial step was one of simple, bold, imaginative engagement. He asked himself: what was it like to be there? Other historians he had read were reluctant to face that question. In Thiers's *Histoire de la Révolution française*, for example, Carlyle found: 'A superficial air of order, of clearness, calm candour, is spread over the work; but inwardly, it is waste, inorganic; no human head that honestly tries can conceive the French Revolution *so*.'[6] In Mignet's book he had noticed 'a compactness, a rigour, as of riveted rods of iron: this also is an image of what symmetry it has; —symmetry, if not of a living earth-born Tree, yet of a firm well-manufactured Gridiron. Without life, without colour or verdure…'[7] Worse even than the French were the English histories: 'copious if not in facts, yet in reflections on facts… He who wishes to know how a solid *Custos rotulorum*, speculating over his port after dinner, interprets the phenomena of contemporary Universal History, may look in these books: he who does not wish that, need not look.'[8] In sharp contrast, Carlyle set out to write

3

a vividly imagined living history with an organic structure suited to the unfolding of the events themselves. He did not doubt the difficulty of his undertaking and, for all his self-proclaimed exceptionalism, he knew there was a fighting chance he would join the ranks of those who had taken up the challenge of the Revolution only to give consciously 'some poor crotchety picture of several things' and unconsciously a picture of themselves, while 'the Phenomenon, for its part, subsists there, all the while, unaltered; waiting to be pictured as often as you like, its entire meaning not to be compressed into any picture drawn by man.'[9]

The idea for Carlyle's book grew from his friendship with John Stuart Mill. In 1833, Mill had written a review of the first two volumes of Alison's *Europe during the French Revolution* in the *Monthly Repository*, and Carlyle wrote to him in Paris, approving of the review and encouraging him to set down his own ideas on the Revolution at greater length:

> *Understand* me all those sectionary tumults, convention-harangues, guillotine holocausts, Brunswick discom-fitures; exhaust me the meaning of it! You *cannot*; for it is a flaming *Reality*; the depths of Eternity look thro' the *chinks* of that so *convulsed* section of Time;—as thro *all* sections of Time, only to dull eyes not so visibly. To me, it often seems, as if the right *History* (that impossible thing I mean by History) of the French Revolution were the grand Poem of our Time; as if the man who *could* write the *truth* of that, were worth all other writers and singers. If I were spared alive myself, and had means, why might not I too prepare the way for such a thing? I assure you the attempt often seems among

my possibilities. The attempt *can* be made; cannot, by the highest talent and effort, be succeeded in, except in more or less feeble approximation. But indeed is not all our success approximate only?— In any case I continue thoroughly interested in the subject, and greedily collect whatever knowledge I can of it.[10]

So continued Carlyle's voracious reading on the subject. Even at this early stage, the structure of his narrative was foreshadowed in his phrasing 'sectionary tumults', 'convention-harangues' and 'guillotine holocausts'. When he began to write in September 1834, Carlyle hoped to finish his history of the Revolution quickly and in just one volume. By the beginning of 1835, he had accepted that it would take three, whose titles turned out to be: *The Bastille*, *The Constitution*, *The Guillotine*.[11] Modern editions of *The French Revolution* typically publish all three volumes in one. As a result the volume headings get lost among the plethora of Carlyle's flamboyant chapter and section headings. This is a shame because rarely has the division of volumes proved so consequential.

In February 1835, when Carlyle reached the end of his first volume, *The Bastille*, Mill offered to read it for him. All along, Mill had been supplying Carlyle with books on the Revolution, and he offered to make notes on the manuscript that might be included as footnotes. On the night of 6 March, Mill arrived on the Carlyle's doorstep, semi-coherent and deeply distraught. There had been a domestic accident and Carlyle's 'poor manuscript, all except some four tattered leaves, was annihilated!'[12] Allegedly, a servant either at Mill's house, or at his mistress Harriet Taylor's, had mistaken *The*

Bastille for waste paper and put it into the fire. That night in bed Carlyle suffered the symptoms of a heart attack, feeling 'something cutting or hard grasping me round the heart.'[13] He dreamt of death and graves, but in the morning he wrote to his publisher Fraser to explain what had happened and resolved to try again. The labour of five steadfast months had 'vanished irrecoverably; worse than if it had never been!'[14] With astonishing resignation, Carlyle wrote, 'I can be angry with no one; for they that were concerned in it have a far deeper sorrow than mine: it is purely the hand of Providence; and, by the blessing of Providence, I must struggle to take it as such… *That* first volume (which pleased me better than anything I had ever done) *cannot* be written anew, for the spirit that animated it is past: but *another* first volume I will try, and shall make it, if not better or equal, *all* that I can. This only is clear to me: that I *can* write a Book on the French Revolution; and that, if I am spared long enough alive I will do it.'[15] Previously, Fraser had suggested publishing the first volume alone, but Carlyle, fearing the lure of idleness, had refused to let it appear before the others were written; now there was next to nothing left.

At the time of the burning, Carlyle was close to completing the opening section of the second volume, 'The Feast of Pikes'. By the end of March it was finished, and he made a point of giving it to Mill to read, attesting his trust in his friend despite everything. Then, after hesitating as to whether to go back or forwards, he opted for the former and began the terrible task of rewriting what had been destroyed. It took until the end of September: six months to complete the 'ugliest task ever set me'.[16] After just a few weeks, Carlyle thought he could not go on, and collapsed on the sofa reading 'the trashiest heap of novels'.[17] But by August he could write to another friend, George Ripley, reassuring him that 'the burnt ashes have again grown *leaves* after a sort'.[18] The writing of the second volume, *The Constitution*, took from November 1835 to the end of April 1836. At this point, during the 'interregnum', as he called the short lapse of time before he began volume three, Carlyle allowed himself to write a review of the *Histoire Parlementaire de la Révolution Française*, that he had promised Mill. Mill published it in the *London and Westminster Review* in 1837.[19] In his review Carlyle records and comments on the most important sources for his work in progress. Among all the writings on the Revolution 'the weight of which would sink an Indiaman', he rated only four 'as forwarding essentially a right knowledge of this matter'. First, the *Analyse du Moniteur* (complete with the expository index of *Le Moniteur* newspaper from 1789–99, and the series of a hundred portraits published with the original edition); second, the *Choix des Rapports, Opinions et Discours* (some 20 volumes of speeches, etc., excellently indexed); third, a collection of revolutionary *Memoirs* that ran to over a hundred volumes, especially the two volumes devoted to memoirs of the prisons; and fourth, the *Histoire Parlementaire* that was under review. Of this last, Carlyle remarked: 'No livelier emblem of the time, in its actual movement and tumult could be presented.'

In his review, Carlyle quoted a long passage from the *Histoire Parlementaire* on the September Massacres which followed the final collapse of the monarchy in August 1792. The victims were mostly prisoners – women, children and priests among them – who had been arrested in an atmosphere of panic as the Duke of Brunswick, at the head of the émigré forces, threatened to reach Paris and extinguish the Revolution. Instead, the so-called 'people's justice' let the blood of the cornered prisoners flow, while the city's Commune, or revolutionary government, stood by and watched it happen. From the *Histoire Parlementaire*, Carlyle extracted an eye-witness account of the people's justice in action:

They run thither: in five minutes more, I saw them trailing corpses by the heels. A killer (I cannot say a man), in very coarse clothes, had, as it would seem, been specially commissioned to despatch the Abbé Lenfant; for, apprehensive lest the prey might be missed, he takes water, flings it on the corpses, washes their blood-smeared faces, turns them over, and seems at last to ascertain that the Abbé Lenfant is among them.[20]

He gives this as an example of how scene after scene discloses itself in the *Histoire Parlementaire*, 'now in rose-light, now in sulphurous black' growing ever more fitful and dreamlike, 'as in some Ezekiel Vision become real'. In the review, Carlyle was describing and illustrating his experience as a reader; in his book, he transformed that experience into frenetic prose intended to reproduce in his readers the impact the original sources had on himself. After the review was finished, Carlyle settled down to write the third and darkest volume of his history, *The Guillotine*. The title of its first book was simply *September*. Drawing on what he had read in the *Histoire Parlementaire* and elsewhere, Carlyle pictured Satan burst forth upon the earth and 'actions of such emphasis that no shrieking can be too emphatic for them':

> This is the September Massacre, otherwise called 'Severe Justice of the People.' These are the Septemberers (Septembriseurs); a name of some note and lucency, —but lucency of the Nether-fire sort; very different from that of our Bastille Heroes, who shone, disputable by no Friend of Freedom, as in heavenly light-radiance: to such phasis of the business have we advanced since then![21]

By July 1836 Carlyle claimed to have only a hundred pages of his book left to write; by November he was 'within forty-five pages of the end', and hoping to be finished on New Year's Day.[22] It was late in the evening of 12 January when he got there.

This edition presents extracts from each of the three volumes, beginning with the famous procession that opened the Estates General, France's largest representative body comprising the Clergy, Nobility and Commons (or Third Estate), in Versailles on 4 May 1789. Carlyle invites the reader to join him in watching the procession with 'prophetic' eyes. He picks out the faces in the crowd that have a florid revolutionary future ahead of them. Of these, Mirabeau and Robespierre are the most important. Gabriel Honoré Riquetti de Mirabeau was destined to become the unofficial leader of the Commons. Unlike most of the deputies assembled to represent the Third Estate, he had a pre-revolutionary reputation: he had been a man of letters, journalist, pornographer, seducer, and prisoner alongside the Marquis de Sade in the Bastille. The nobility rejected Mirabeau as one of their representatives, so he stood for the commons instead. Carlyle latches onto him and warns the reader 'mark him well'. Just as Louis XIV once claimed '*L'état c'est moi*', Mirabeau might have said, 'The National Assembly? I am that.' The contrast with the unknown lawyer from Arras, Maximilien Robespierre, is deliberately drawn:

> But now if Mirabeau is the greatest, who of these Six Hundred may be the meanest?' Shall we say, that anxious, slight, ineffectual-looking man, under thirty, in spectacles; his eyes (were the glasses off) troubled, careful; with upturned face, snuffing dimly the uncertain future-time; complexion of a multiplex atrabiliar colour, the final shade of which may be the pale sea-green.[23]

Richard Cobb argued that Carlyle 'approaches the Revolution in search of a Hero'.[24] Mirabeau is his best, if wholly unsatisfactory, candidate for heroism until he dies suddenly in 1791, but Robespierre is Carlyle's definitive anti-hero.

After the procession at the opening of the Estates General, volume one covers two major turning points in the early phase of the Revolution: the Tennis Court Oath, at which the Third Estate proclaimed itself the National Assembly with the right to design a new constitution for France, and the fall of the Bastille on 14 July 1789. The latter exasperates Carlyle and he complains that it is a task that 'perhaps transcends the talent of mortals': after copious reading he can hardly get a plan of the building in his head. The words,

'Let conflagration rage; of whatever is combustible' are poignant in the context of the burnt manuscript that Carlyle was writing to replace. He has brilliant visual sense, cutting, for example, from the flow of blood outside the prison walls to the great Bastille clock in its inner court, ticking at its ease 'as if nothing special, for it or the world, were passing!' After the action is all over, he pauses to consider 'what precisely these two words, French Revolution, shall mean; for, strictly considered, they may have as many meanings as there are speakers of them.'

Carlyle's answer to this question is revealing of his narrative purpose:

For ourselves we answer that French Revolution means here the open violent Rebellion, and Victory, of disimprisoned Anarchy against corrupt worn-out Authority: how Anarchy breaks prison; bursts up from the infinite Deep, and rages uncontrollable, immeasurable, enveloping a world; in phasis after phasis of fever-frenzy; —'till the frenzy burning itself out, and what elements of new Order it held (since all Force holds such) developing themselves, the Uncontrollable be got, if not reimprisoned, yet harnessed, and its mad forces made to work towards their object as sane regulated ones.[25]

From Edmund Burke to Simon Schama, many commentators on the Revolution have depicted it as an unnecessary and gratuitously bloody mistake.[26] Carlyle is not among them. For him it was a transcendental phenomenon, 'the world-Phoenix, in fire-consummation and fire creation... the Death-Birth of a World!'[27] To ask where it came from, or where it was going, was to pose unmanageable questions. Instead of analyzing, or explaining – forlorn tasks in the circumstances, or so it seemed to him – Carlyle set himself to evoke and describe. At the end of volume one, he pictures in apocalyptical terms SANSCULOTTISM, rising up amid Tartarean smoke, many-headed, fire-breathing, and asking: what think ye of me? Thus he makes an unknowable monster of the figure of the *sans-culotte*, more commonly identified with the popular movement, or participation of ordinary people in the Revolution.

In his second volume, Carlyle describes the celebrations in Paris for the first anniversary of the fall of the Bastille: the Champ-de-Mars Federation, which he christens 'The Feast of Pikes'. Here again, his eye catches tiny telling details. As Talleyrand, Bishop of Autun, climbed the steps of the Altar of the Fatherland to officiate, the skies opened and there was a downpour of rain. Carlyle notices the crowd's snowy muslins all splashed and bedraggled and a single ostrich feather 'shrunk shamefully to the backbone of a feather'. He creates the illusion that he was there watching the rainfall.[28] Later he compares the festival that ostensibly celebrated Louis XVI's acceptance of the Revolution, to a fond but foolish wedding at which, amid fireworks and celebrations, the elderly shook their heads knowingly because it was to be a bitterly unhappy marriage. Less than a year on from the Festival of Federation, the relationship between the nation and Louis XVI was all but unworkable. Mirabeau was the only hope for fixing it, and Mirabeau was dying, he 'could not live another year, any more than he could live another thousand years.'[29] He died on 2 April 1791. Carlyle was not the first or last to speculate that the Revolution would have taken a different course if he had lived.

The constitutional monarchy that finally came into effect at the end of September 1791 was the product of two years' intense discussion, but it was ill-made. From the start, it did not seem likely that the new legislative body and Louis XVI would cooperate in governing France. Carlyle remarks that 'extremely rheumatic Constitutions have been known to march, and keep on their feet, though in a staggering sprawling manner, for long periods, in virtue of one thing only: that the Head were healthy.' He blames Louis XVI for indecision and confusion. Under a year later, the constitutional monarchy collapsed on 10 August 1792. Carlyle captures the atmosphere of that night hauntingly:

> Reader, fancy not, in thy languid way, that Insurrection is easy. Insurrection is difficult: each individual uncertain of his next neighbour; totally uncertain of his distant neighbours, what strength is with him, what strength is against him; certain only that, in case of failure, his individual portion is the gallows![30]

Carlyle's imaginative engagement with the Revolution extended to the passion felt by an unnamed man in the crowd who turned out to invade the Tuileries Palace, and the passion not felt by the indifferent Parisian who went on sleeping. He takes the reader on a flight above the roofs of Paris and lets her see inside them from the height of Notre Dame's tower. There, side by side with courage and fear, is sheer dullness 'calmly snoring'.[31] It is the whole gamut of human emotions in the Revolution, from the hysterical clamour of those that rang the tocsin to blithe unconcern, which interests him. He is always pressing the question:

what was it like to be there? But his perspective is restless, darting in and out of the revolutionary scenes he describes, seeing them from above and below, up close and from afar, through the eyes of the famous and the forgotten. After the invasion of the Tuileries Palace, when the French monarchy was plainly finished, Carlyle imagines the 'silent rage of the Old-Constituents, Constitution-builders... men who thought the Constitution would march.'[32] He focuses on the feelings of the routed as much as on those of the victorious.

The third volume is aptly called *The Guillotine*, since it was after the collapse of the monarchy that the instrument of execution was first set up close to the Tuileries Palace (sometimes in the Place du Carrousel, sometimes on the Place de la Révolution, which is now the Place de la Concorde). The first public use of the invention named after Dr Guillotine, who promoted it in the National Assembly, was 25 April 1792[33], but on that occasion it was used to execute a criminal outside the Hôtel de Ville. Moving the guillotine closer to the Tuileries Palace had ominous symbolism. What was going to happen to Louis XVI? Carlyle remarks that 'it is unfortunate, though very natural, that the history of this Period has so generally been written in hysterics. Exaggeration abounds, execration, wailing; and on the whole, darkness.'[34] It could not be said that he did much to inject calm. He certainly exaggerates and embellishes. Of Robespierre during September 1792, he writes:

> That incorruptible Robespierre is not wanting, now when the brunt of the battle is past; in a stealthy way the seagreen man sits there, his feline eyes excellent in the twilight.[35]

'Poor Robespierre', Richard Cobb remarked, 'who could hardly see in the daylight and who had to wear tinted glasses.'[36] From where, except his imagination, does Carlyle draw the detail that Robespierre, cat-like, could see better in the dark?

But Carlyle is also capable of accurate concision: of conveying, for example, all the complexities of the Convention's voting on Louis XVI's future in the short section 'The Three Votings'. Here too he describes the factional strife beginning between the Mountain and the Girondins, two loose groupings of the deputies to the Convention, destined to fight each other to death over the future of the new Republic. The sentence, 'At home this killing of a King has divided all friends; and abroad it has united all enemies', is a brilliant compression of the domestic and international impact of Louis XVI's trial and execution on 21 January 1793.[37]

A year after the collapse of the monarchy, Paris celebrated with 'a new Feast of Pikes'. Carlyle is at his sneering best in the chapter 'O Nature' that describes the hideous papier-mâché statues of Nature and Liberty 'hoping to become metal', on the site of the razed Bastille and in the Place de la Révolution. Making fun of Jacques-Louis David, the Revolution's portrait painter and stage-set designer, he writes: 'Thanks to David and the French genius, there steps forth into the sunlight, this day, a Scenic Phantasmagory unexampled: —whereof History, so occupied with Real-Phantasmagories, will say but little.'[38] Phantasmagories were a form of theatrical shadow play involving the projection of ghosts onto smoke, popular in France in the late eighteenth century and afterwards in Britain in the nineteenth century.

Carlyle was not alone in applying the concept to the French Revolution. His contemporary, John Wilson Croker, wrote: 'The most important, yet the most mysterious figure in the phantasmagoria of the French Revolution is Maximilien Robespierre. Of no one of whom so much has been said is so little known.'[39] Carlyle was less willing than Croker to draw attention to absence of fact in his narrative; typically, he assembled as many facts as he could find and confidently vivified them. The idea of a real, as opposed to a fictional or invented, phantasmagoria is helpful in gauging Carlyle's approach to history. The story of the Revolution, as he understood it, was 'the march of a red baleful phantasmagoria towards the land of phantoms', but it had been real enough and it was rooted in fact.[40]

When he comes to describe the Terror, Carlyle addresses directly the problem of writing its history. At first, on the subject of the 'Horrors of the French Revolution', there was 'abundance to be said and shrieked.' But these horrors were not the phenomenon itself, only the shadow of it, according to Carlyle. His hope for his own generation was that history would cease shrieking and 'include under her old forms of speech or speculation this new amazing thing.' Historians, however, were disappointing him. Roux, one of the authors of the *Histoire Parlementaire*, that Carlyle esteemed so highly, had recently suggested that the French Revolution was an attempt to realize the Christian religion. Carlyle was indignant:

Alas, no, M. Roux! A Gospel of Brotherhood, not according to any of the Four old Evangelists, and calling on men to repent, and amend each his own wicked

16

existence, that they might be saved; but a Gospel rather, as we often hint, according to a new Fifth Evangelist Jean-Jacques, calling on men to amend each the whole world's wicked existence, and be saved by making the Constitution.[41]

Carlyle's hatred of Rousseau, and contempt for the role the ideas and followers of Rousseau played in the Revolution, runs throughout his book. His advice to his fellow historians was to accept that the unprecedented phenomenon of the Revolution had unveiled new laws of nature that could not be described using old names and theories. For the time being, historians should drop the pretence of definitively naming or describing the Revolution, and look at it instead honestly, naming only such components as they could, in a piecemeal fashion. He could see nothing constructive in it, only Rousseau's gospel disastrously applied as a theorem that became a creed and in the process destroyed everything susceptible of destruction:

What then is this Thing, called La Révolution which, like an Angel of Death, hangs over France, noyading, fusillading, fighting, gun-boring, tanning human skins? La Révolution is but so many Alphabetic Letters; a thing nowhere to be laid hands on, to be clapt under lock and key: where is it? What is it? It is the Madness that dwells in the hearts of men.[42]

The final short section, *Finis*, begins by reminding the reader that Homer's Epic, like a bas-relief sculpture, does not conclude, but merely ceases. Carlyle, accordingly, attempts no concluding remarks: he has already shown us all he can of the Revolution, and there is nothing further he can say. Yet he cannot resist a fond leave-taking, reflecting that the journey we have been on with him has been toilsome, but sacred, because 'while the Voice of Man speaks with Man, hast thou not there the living fountain out of which all sacredness sprang, and will yet spring?'[43] It is because his voice speaks so distinctively and directly through his text that Carlyle's is still the most exciting account of the Revolution there has ever been.

Ruth Scurr

SUGGESTIONS FOR FURTHER READING

Ben-Israel, Hedva, *English Historians of the French Revolution*, (Cambridge: Cambridge University Press, 1968).

Croker, John Wilson, *Essays on the Early Period of the French Revolution (1857)*, (Montana: Kessinger Publishing Co., 2009).

Kaplan, Fred, *Thomas Carlyle: A Biography*, (Ithaca: Cornell University Press, 1983).

Michelet, Jules, *History of the French Revolution* (1847–53), translated by Charles Cocks, edited and with an introduction by Gordon Wright, (Chicago: University of Chicago Press, 1967).

Palmer, R. R., *Twelve Who Ruled: the Year of the Terror in the French Revolution*, (Princeton: Princeton University Press, 1970).

Young, Brian, *The Victorian Eighteenth Century: An Intellectual History*, (Oxford: Oxford University Press, 2007).

NOTES

1. *Carlyle Letters Online* (CLO), Thomas Carlyle to John Sterling; 17 January 1837; DOI: 10.1215/lt-18370117-TC-JOST-01; *CL* 9: 115–120.

2. ibid.

3. ibid.

4. *Sartor Resartus* (1833–4), republished in *The Centenary Edition of the Works of Thomas Carlyle*, ed. H. D.Traill, 30 vols, London 1896–98.

5. *Thomas Carlyle: A Biography*, F. Kaplan, Ithaca: Cornell University Press, 1983, p. 217.

6. *Critical and Miscellaneous Essays*, collected and republished, by Thomas Carlyle, London: Chapman & Hall, 1847, vol. 4, p. 79. See also A. Thiers, *Histoire de la Révolution française*, 8 vols, Paris: Furne, 1846–66 (first published in 10 vols, 1823–27).

7. ibid. See also M. Mignet, *Histoire de la Révolution française: depuis 1789 jusqu'au 1814*, London: David Nutt, 1894 (first published 1824).

8. *Critical and Miscellaneous Essays*, vol. 4, p. 82.

9. *Critical and Miscellaneous Essays*, vol. 4, p. 78.

10. Thomas Carlyle to John Stuart Mill; 24 September 1833; DOI: 10.1215/lt-18330924-TC-JSM-01; *CL* 6: 444–50.

11. Thomas Carlyle to William Graham; 10 January 1835; DOI: 10.1215/lt-18350110-TC-WG-01; *CL* 8: 5–6.

12. *Thomas Carlyle: A Biography*, p. 218.

13. *Thomas Carlyle: A Biography*, p. 219.

14. Thomas Carlyle to James Fraser; 7 March 1835, DOI: 10.1215/lt-18350307-TC-JFR-01; *CL* 8: 66–70.

15. ibid.

16. Thomas Carlyle to George Ripley; 12 August 1835; DOI: 10.1215/lt-18350800-TC-GRI-01; *CL* 8: 191–92.

17. Thomas Carlyle to Margaret A. Carlyle; 1 May 1835; DOI: 10.1215/lt-18350501-TC-MAC-01; *CL* 8: 108–13. The novelist Carlyle specifically mentions reading at this time is Frederick Marryat (1792–1848).

18. Thomas Carlyle to George Ripley; 12 August 1835; DOI: 10.1215/lt-18350800-TC-GRI-01; *CL* 8: 191–92.

19. Thomas Carlyle to John Stuart Mill; 2 May 1836; DOI: 10.1215/lt-18360502-TC-JSM-01; *CL* 8: 338–40; Carlyle's 'Parliamentary History of the French Revolution,' was published by Mill in the *London and Westminster Review*, XXVII (April 1837), 233–47; republished in *Critical and Miscellaneous Essays*, collected and republished, London: Chapman & Hall, 1847, vol. 4, pp. 77–98.

20. *Critical and Miscellaneous Essays*, vol. 4, p. 97.

21. ibid, vol. 3, p. 163 (below p. 125).

22. *Thomas Carlyle: A Biography*, p. 222.

23. *The French Revolution: A History*, Thomas Carlyle, ed. K. J. Fielding and D. Sorensen, Oxford: Oxford University Press, 1989, 3 vols published in one, vol. 1, p. 148 (below p. 33).

24. *The French Revolution: A History*, introduced by Richard Cobb, London: The Folio Society, 1989, p. xv.

25. *The French Revolution: A History*, vol. 1, p. 221 (below p. 61).

26. *Reflections on the Revolution in France*, E. Burke (1790), ed. J. G. A. Pocock, Indianapolis: Hackett: L, 1987; *Citizens: A Chronicle of the French Revolution*, S. Schama, London: Penguin, 2004.

27. *The French Revolution: A History*, vol. 1, p.223 (below p. 63).

28. *The French Revolution: A History*, vol. 1, p. 369.

29. *The French Revolution: A History*, vol. 1, p. 445 (below p. 72).

30. *The French Revolution: A History*, vol. 2, p. 102 (below p. 88).

31. *The French Revolution: A History*, vol. 2, p. 103 (below p. 88).

32. *The French Revolution: A History*, vol. 2, p. 118.

33. *Archives Parlementaire de 1787 à 1860, Débats législatifs et Politiques des chambres Français*, sous la direction de M. J. Mavidal et de M. E. Laurent, Première Série, 1787–99, 82 vols, Paris (1885): Libraire administrative de Paul Dupont, vol. 26, p. 332.

34. *The French Revolution: A History*, vol. 3, p. 124 (below p. 108).

35. *The French Revolution: A History*, vol. 3, p. 129 (below p. 110).

36. *The French Revolution: A History*, introduced by Richard Cobb, London: The Folio Society, 1989, p. xiv.

37. *The French Revolution: A History*, vol. 3, p. 237 (below p. 140).

38. *The French Revolution: A History*, vol .3, p. 309 (below p. 156).

39. *Essays on the Early Period of the French Revolution (reprinted from the Quarterly Review with additions and corrections)*, J. W. Croker, London: John Murray, 1857, p. 299.

40. *The French Revolution: A History*, vol. 3, p .399 (below p. 183). See also, 'Phantasmagoria: Spectral Technology and the Metaphorics of Modern Reverie', T. Castle in *Critical Inquiry*, Chicago: University of Chicago Press, vol. 15, no. 1 (Autumn, 1988), pp. 26–61.

41. *The French Revolution: A History*, vol. 3, p. 333 (below p. 165).

42. *The French Revolution: A History*, vol. 3, p. 377 (below p. 169).

43. *The French Revolution: A History*, vol. 3, p. 453 (below p. 195).

THE FRENCH
REVOLUTION

PART I – THE BASTILLE

THE PROCESSION

1789

But now finally the Sun, on Monday the 4th of May, has risen; – unconcerned, as if it were no special day. And yet, as his first rays could strike music from the Memnon's Statue on the Nile, what tones were these, so thrilling, tremulous of preparation and foreboding, which he awoke in every bosom at Versailles! Huge Paris, in all conceivable and inconceivable vehicles, is pouring itself forth; from each Town and Village come subsidiary rills; Versailles is a very sea of men. But above all, from the Church of St. Louis to the Church of Notre-Dame: one vast suspended-billow of Life, – with spray scattered even to the chimney-pots! For on chimney-tops too, as over the roofs, and up thitherwards on every lamp-iron, sign-post, breakneck coign of vantage, sits patriotic Courage; and every window bursts with patriotic Beauty: for the Deputies are gathering at St. Louis Church; to march in procession to Notre-Dame, and hear sermon.

Yes, friends, ye may sit and look: boldly or in thought, all France, and all Europe, may sit and look; for it is a day like few others. Oh, one might weep like Xerxes: – So many serried rows sit perched there; like winged creatures, alighted out of Heaven: all these, and so many more that follow them, shall have wholly fled aloft again, vanishing into the blue

27

Deep; and the memory of this day still be fresh. It is the baptism-day of Democracy; sick Time has given it birth, the numbered months being run. The extreme-unction day of Feudalism! A superannuated System of Society, decrepit with toils (for has it not done much; produced you, and what ye have and know!) – and with thefts and brawls, named glorious-victories; and with profligacies, sensualities, and on the whole with dotage and senility, – is now to die: and so, with death-throes and birth-throes, a new one is to be born. What a work, O Earth and Heavens, what a work! Battles and bloodshed, September Massacres, Bridges of Lodi, retreats of Moscow, Waterloos, Peterloos, Tenpound Franchises, Tarbarrels and Guillotines; – and from this present date, if one might prophesy, some two centuries of it still to fight! Two centuries; hardly less; before Democracy go through its due, most baleful, stages of Quackocracy; and a pestilential World be burnt up, and have begun to grow green and young again.

Rejoice nevertheless, ye Versailles multitudes; to you, from whom all this is hid, and glorious end of it is visible. This day, sentence of death is pronounced on Shams; judgment of resuscitation, were it but far off, is pronounced on Realities. This day it is declared aloud, as with a Doom-trumpet, that a Lie is unbelievable. Believe that, stand by that, if more there be not; and let what thing or things soever will follow it follow. 'Ye can no other; God be your help!' So spake a greater than any of you; opening his Chapter of World-History.

Behold, however! The doors of St. Louis Church flung wide; and the Procession of Processions advancing towards Notre-Dame! Shouts rend the air; one shout, at which

Grecian birds might drop dead. It is indeed a stately, solemn sight. The Elected of France, and then the Court of France; they are marshalled and march there, all in prescribed place and costume. Our Commons 'in plain black mantle and white cravat;' Noblesse, in gold-worked, bright-dyed cloaks of velvet, resplendent, rustling with laces, waving with plumes; the Clergy in rochet, alb, or other best pontificalibus: lastly comes the King himself, and King's Household, also in their brightest blaze of pomp, – their brightest and final one. Some Fourteen Hundred Men blown together from all winds, on the deepest errand.

Yes, in that silent marching mass there lies Futurity enough. No symbolic Ark, like the old Hebrews, do these men bear: yet with them too is a Covenant; they too preside at a new Era in the History of Men. The whole Future is there, and Destiny dim-brooding over it; in the hearts and unshaped thoughts of these men, it lies illegible, inevitable. Singular to think: they have it in them; yet not they, not mortal, only the Eye above can read it, – as it shall unfold itself, in fire and thunder, of siege, and field-artillery; in the rustling of battle-banners, the tramp of hosts, in the glow of burning cities, the shriek of strangled nations! Such things lie hidden, safe-wrapt in this Fourth day of May; – say rather, had lain in some other unknown day, of which this latter is the public fruit and outcome. As indeed what wonders lie in every Day, – had we the sight, as happily we have not, to decipher it: for is not every meanest Day 'the conflux of two Eternities!'

Meanwhile, suppose we too, good Reader, should, as now without miracle Muse Clio enables us – take our station also on some coign of vantage; and glance momentarily over this

Procession, and this Life-sea; with far other eyes than the rest do, namely with prophetic? We can mount, and stand there, without fear of falling.

As for the Life-sea, or onlooking unnumbered Multitude, it is unfortunately all-too dim. Yet as we gaze fixedly, do not nameless Figures not a few, which shall not always be nameless, disclose themselves; visible or presumable there! Young Baroness de Stael – she evidently looks from a window; among older honourable women. Her father is Minister, and one of the gala personages; to his own eyes the chief one. Young spiritual Amazon, thy rest is not there; nor thy loved Father's: 'as Malebranche saw all things in God, so M. Necker sees all things in Necker,' – a theorem that will not hold.

But where is the brown-locked, light-behaved, fire-hearted Demoiselle Theroigne? Brown eloquent Beauty; who, with thy winged words and glances, shalt thrill rough bosoms, whole steel battalions, and persuade an Austrian Kaiser, – pike and helm lie provided for thee in due season; and, alas, also strait-waistcoat and long lodging in the Salpetriere! Better hadst thou staid in native Luxemburg, and been the mother of some brave man's children: but it was not thy task, it was not thy lot.

Surely also, in some place not of honour, stands or sprawls up querulous, that he too, though short, may see, – one squalidest bleared mortal, redolent of soot and horse-drugs: Jean Paul Marat of Neuchatel! O Marat, Renovator of Human Science, Lecturer on Optics; O thou remarkablest Horseleech, once in D'Artois' Stables, – as thy bleared soul looks forth, through thy bleared, dull-acrid, wo-stricken face, what sees it in all this? Any faintest light of hope; like dayspring after Nova-Zembla night? Or is it but blue sulphur-light, and spectres; woe, suspicion, revenge without end?

Two other Figures, and only two, we signalise there. The huge, brawny, Figure; through whose black brows, and rude flattened face (figure ecrasee), there looks a waste energy as of Hercules not yet furibund, – he is an esurient, unprovided Advocate; Danton by name: him mark. Then that other, his slight-built comrade and craft-brother; he with the long curling locks; with the face of dingy blackguardism, wondrously irradiated with genius, as if a naphtha-lamp burnt within it: that Figure is Camille Desmoulins. A fellow of infinite shrewdness, wit, nay humour; one of the sprightliest clearest souls in all these millions. Thou poor Camille, say of thee what they may, it were but falsehood to pretend one did not almost love thee, thou headlong lightly-sparkling man! But the brawny, not yet furibund Figure, we say, is Jacques Danton; a name that shall be 'tolerably known in the Revolution.' He is President of the electoral Cordeliers District at Paris, or about to be it; and shall open his lungs of brass.

We dwell no longer on the mixed shouting Multitude: for now, behold, the Commons Deputies are at hand!

Which of these Six Hundred individuals, in plain white cravat, that have come up to regenerate France, might one guess would become their king? For a king or leader they, as all bodies of men, must have: be their work what it may, there is one man there who, by character, faculty, position, is fittest of all to do it; that man, as future not yet elected king, walks

31

there among the rest. He with the thick black locks, will it be? With the hure, as himself calls it, or black boar's-head, fit to be 'shaken' as a senatorial portent? Through whose shaggy beetle-brows, and rough-hewn, seamed, carbuncled face, there look natural ugliness, small-pox, incontinence, bankruptcy, – and burning fire of genius; like comet-fire glaring fuliginous through murkiest confusions? It is Gabriel Honore Riquetti de Mirabeau, the world-compeller; man-ruling Deputy of Aix! According to the Baroness de Stael, he steps proudly along, though looked at askance here, and shakes his black chevelure, or lion's-mane; as if prophetic of great deeds.

Yes, Reader, that is the Type-Frenchman of this epoch; as Voltaire was of the last. He is French in his aspirations, acquisitions, in his virtues, in his vices; perhaps more French than any other man; – and intrinsically such a mass of manhood too. Mark him well. The National Assembly were all different without that one; nay, he might say with the old Despot: "The National Assembly? I am that."

Towards such work, in such manner, marches he, this singular Riquetti Mirabeau. In fiery rough figure, with black Samson-locks under the slouch-hat, he steps along there. A fiery fuliginous mass, which could not be choked and smothered, but would fill all France with smoke. And now it has got air; it will burn its whole substance, its whole smoke-atmosphere too, and fill all France with flame. Strange lot! Forty years of that smouldering, with foul fire-damp and vapour enough, then victory over that; – and like a burning mountain he blazes heaven-high; and, for twenty-three resplendent months, pours out, in flame and molten fire-torrents, all that is in him, the Pharos and Wonder-sign of an amazed Europe; – and then lies hollow, cold forever! Pass on, thou questionable Gabriel Honore, the greatest of them all: in the whole National Deputies, in the whole Nation, there is none like and none second to thee.

But now if Mirabeau is the greatest, who of these Six Hundred may be the meanest? Shall we say, that anxious, slight, ineffectual-looking man, under thirty, in spectacles; his eyes (were the glasses off) troubled, careful; with upturned face, snuffing dimly the uncertain future-time; complexion of a multiplex atrabiliar colour, the final shade of which may be the pale sea-green. That greenish-coloured (verdatre) individual is an Advocate of Arras; his name is Maximilien Robespierre. The son of an Advocate; his father founded mason-lodges under Charles Edward, the English Prince or Pretender. Maximilien the first-born was thriftily educated; he had brisk Camille Desmoulins for schoolmate in the College of Louis le Grand, at Paris. But he begged our famed Necklace-Cardinal, Rohan, the patron, to let him depart thence, and resign in favour of a younger brother. The strict-minded Max departed; home to paternal Arras; and even had a Law-case there and pleaded, not unsuccessfully, 'in favour of the first Franklin thunder-rod.' With a strict painful mind, an understanding small but clear and ready, he grew in favour with official persons, who could foresee in him an excellent man of business, happily quite free from genius. The Bishop, therefore, taking counsel, appoints him Judge of his diocese; and he faithfully does justice to the people: till behold, one day, a culprit comes whose crime merits hanging; and the strict-minded Max must abdicate, for his conscience will not permit the dooming of any son of

Adam to die. A strict-minded, strait-laced man! A man unfit for Revolutions? Whose small soul, transparent wholesome-looking as small ale, could by no chance ferment into virulent alegar, – the mother of ever new alegar; till all France were grown acetous virulent? We shall see.

Between which two extremes of grandest and meanest, so many grand and mean roll on, towards their several destinies, in that Procession!

And worthy Doctor Guillotin, whom we hoped to behold one other time? If not here, the Doctor should be here, and we see him with the eye of prophecy: for indeed the Parisian Deputies are all a little late. Singular Guillotin, respectable practitioner: doomed by a satiric destiny to the strangest immortal glory that ever kept obscure mortal from his resting-place, the bosom of oblivion! Guillotin can improve the ventilation of the Hall; in all cases of medical police and hygiene be a present aid: but, greater far, he can produce his 'Report on the Penal Code;' and reveal therein a cunningly devised Beheading Machine, which shall become famous and world-famous. This is the product of Guillotin's endeavours, gained not without meditation and reading; which product popular gratitude or levity christens by a feminine derivative name, as if it were his daughter: La Guillotine! "With my machine, Messieurs, I whisk off your head (vous fais sauter la tete) in a twinkling, and you have no pain;" – whereat they all laugh. Unfortunate Doctor! For two-and-twenty years he, unguillotined, shall hear nothing but guillotine, see nothing but guillotine; then dying, shall through long centuries wander, as it were, a disconsolate ghost, on the wrong side of Styx and Lethe; his name like to outlive Caesar's.

See Bailly, likewise of Paris, time-honoured Historian of Astronomy Ancient and Modern. Poor Bailly, how thy serenely beautiful Philosophising, with its soft moonshiny clearness and thinness, ends in foul thick confusion – of Presidency, Mayorship, diplomatic Officiality, rabid Triviality, and the throat of everlasting Darkness! Far was it to descend from the heavenly Galaxy to the Drapeau Rouge: beside that fatal dung-heap, on that last hell-day, thou must 'tremble,' though only with cold, 'de froid.' Speculation is not practice: to be weak is not so miserable; but to be weaker than our task. Wo the day when they mounted thee, a peaceable pedestrian, on that wild Hippogriff of a Democracy; which, spurning the firm earth, nay lashing at the very stars, no yet known Astolpho could have ridden!

In the Commons Deputies there are Merchants, Artists, Men of Letters; three hundred and seventy-four Lawyers; and at least one Clergyman: the Abbe Sieyes. Him also Paris sends, among its twenty. Behold him, the light thin man; cold, but elastic, wiry; instinct with the pride of Logic; passionless, or with but one passion, that of self-conceit. If indeed that can be called a passion, which, in its independent concentrated greatness, seems to have soared into transcendentalism; and to sit there with a kind of godlike indifference, and look down on passion! He is the man, and wisdom shall die with him. This is the Sieyes who shall be System-builder, Constitution-builder General; and build Constitutions (as many as wanted) skyhigh, – which shall all unfortunately fall before he get the scaffolding away. "La Politique," said he to Dumont, "Polity is a science I think I have completed (achevee)." What things, O Sieyes, with thy clear assiduous eyes, art thou to see! But were it not curious to know how

35

Sieyes, now in these days (for he is said to be still alive) (A.D. 1834.) looks out on all that Constitution masonry, through the rheumy soberness of extreme age? Might we hope, still with the old irrefragable transcendentalism? The victorious cause pleased the gods, the vanquished one pleased Sieyes (victa Catoni).

Thus, however, amid skyrending vivats, and blessings from every heart, has the Procession of the Commons Deputies rolled by.

Next follow the Noblesse, and next the Clergy; concerning both of whom it might be asked, What they specially have come for? Specially, little as they dream of it, to answer this question, put in a voice of thunder: What are you doing in God's fair Earth and Task-garden; where whosoever is not working is begging or stealing? Wo, wo to themselves and to all, if they can only answer: Collecting tithes, Preserving game! –

There then walks our French Noblesse. All in the old pomp of chivalry: and yet, alas, how changed from the old position; drifted far down from their native latitude, like Arctic icebergs got into the Equatorial sea, and fast thawing there! Once these Chivalry Duces (Dukes, as they are still named) did actually lead the world, – were it only towards battle-spoil, where lay the world's best wages then: moreover, being the ablest Leaders going, they had their lion's share, those Duces; which none could grudge them. But now, when so many Looms, improved Ploughshares, Steam-Engines and Bills of Exchange have been invented; and, for battle-brawling itself, men hire Drill-Sergeants at eighteen-pence a-day, – what mean these goldmantled Chivalry Figures, walking there 'in black-velvet cloaks,' in high-plumed 'hats of a feudal cut'? Reeds shaken in the wind!

The Clergy have got up; with Cahiers for abolishing pluralities, enforcing residence of bishops, better payment of tithes. The Dignitaries, we can observe, walk stately, apart from the numerous Undignified, – who indeed are properly little other than Commons disguised in Curate-frocks. Here, however, though by strange ways, shall the Precept be fulfilled, and they that are greatest (much to their astonishment) become least.

But yonder, halting lamely along, thou noticest next Bishop Talleyrand-Perigord, his Reverence of Autun. A sardonic grimness lies in that irreverent Reverence of Autun. He will do and suffer strange things; and will become surely one of the strangest things ever seen, or like to be seen. A man living in falsehood, and on falsehood; yet not what you can call a false man: there is the specialty! It will be an enigma for future ages, one may hope: hitherto such a product of Nature and Art was possible only for this age of ours, – Age of Paper, and of the Burning of Paper. Consider Bishop Talleyrand and Marquis Lafayette as the topmost of their two kinds; and say once more, looking at what they did and what they were, O Tempus ferax rerum!

On the whole, however, has not this unfortunate Clergy also drifted in the Time-stream, far from its native latitude? An anomalous mass of men; of whom the whole world has already a dim understanding that it can understand nothing. They were once a Priesthood, interpreters of Wisdom, revealers of the Holy that is in Man: a true Clerus (or Inheritance of God on Earth): but now? – They pass silently, with such Cahiers as they have been able to redact; and none cries, God bless them.

King Louis with his Court brings up the rear: he cheerful, in this day of hope, is saluted with plaudits; still more Necker his Minister. Not so the Queen; on whom hope shines not steadily any more. Ill-fated Queen! Her hair is already gray with many cares and crosses; her first-born son is dying in these weeks: black falsehood has ineffaceably soiled her name; ineffaceably while this generation lasts. Instead of Vive la Reine, voices insult her with Vive d'Orleans. Of her queenly beauty little remains except its stateliness; not now gracious, but haughty, rigid, silently enduring. With a most mixed feeling, wherein joy has no part, she resigns herself to a day she hoped never to have seen. Poor Marie Antoinette; with thy quick noble instincts; vehement glancings, vision all-too fitful narrow for the work thou hast to do! O there are tears in store for thee; bitterest wailings, soft womanly meltings, though thou hast the heart of an imperial Theresa's Daughter. Thou doomed one, shut thy eyes on the future! –

And so, in stately Procession, have passed the Elected of France. Some towards honour and quick fire-consummation; most towards dishonour; not a few towards massacre, confusion, emigration, desperation: all towards Eternity! – So many heterogeneities cast together into the fermenting-vat; there, with incalculable action, counteraction, elective affinities, explosive developments, to work out healing for a sick moribund System of Society! Probably the strangest Body of Men, if we consider well, that ever met together on our Planet on such an errand. So thousandfold complex a Society, ready to burst-up from its infinite depths; and these men, its rulers and healers, without life-rule for themselves,

– other life-rule than a Gospel according to Jean Jacques! To the wisest of them, what we must call the wisest, man is properly an Accident under the sky. Man is without Duty round him; except it be 'to make the Constitution.' He is without Heaven above him, or Hell beneath him; he has no God in the world.

What further or better belief can be said to exist in these Twelve Hundred? Belief in high-plumed hats of a feudal cut; in heraldic scutcheons; in the divine right of Kings, in the divine right of Game-destroyers. Belief, or what is still worse, canting half-belief; or worst of all, mere Macchiavellic pretence-of-belief, – in consecrated dough-wafers, and the godhood of a poor old Italian Man! Nevertheless in that immeasurable Confusion and Corruption, which struggles there so blindly to become less confused and corrupt, there is, as we said, this one salient point of a New Life discernible: the deep fixed Determination to have done with Shams. A determination, which, consciously or unconsciously, is fixed; which waxes ever more fixed, into very madness and fixed-idea; which in such embodiment as lies provided there, shall now unfold itself rapidly: monstrous, stupendous, unspeakable; new for long thousands of years! – How has the Heaven's light, oftentimes in this Earth, to clothe itself in thunder and electric murkiness; and descend as molten lightning, blasting, if purifying! Nay is it not rather the very murkiness, and atmospheric suffocation, that brings the lightning and the light? The new Evangel, as the old had been, was it to be born in the Destruction of a World?

But how the Deputies assisted at High Mass, and heard sermon, and applauded the preacher, church as it was, when he preached politics; how, next day, with sustained pomp, they are, for the first time, installed in their Salles des Menus (Hall no longer of Amusements), and become a States-General, – readers can fancy for themselves. The King from his estrade, gorgeous as Solomon in all his glory, runs his eye over that majestic Hall; many-plumed, many-glancing; bright-tinted as rainbow, in the galleries and near side spaces, where Beauty sits raining bright influence. Satisfaction, as of one that after long voyaging had got to port, plays over his broad simple face: the innocent King! He rises and speaks, with sonorous tone, a conceivable speech. With which, still more with the succeeding one-hour and two-hour speeches of Garde-des-Sceaux and M. Necker, full of nothing but patriotism, hope, faith, and deficiency of the revenue, – no reader of these pages shall be tried.

We remark only that, as his Majesty, on finishing the speech, put on his plumed hat, and the Noblesse according to custom imitated him, our Tiers-Etat Deputies did mostly, not without a shade of fierceness, in like manner clap-on, and even crush on their slouched hats; and stand there awaiting the issue. Thick buzz among them, between majority and minority of Couvrezvous, Decrouvrez-vous (Hats off, Hats on)! To which his Majesty puts end, by taking off his own royal hat again.

The session terminates without further accident or omen than this; with which, significantly enough, France has opened her States-General.

INERTIA.

That exasperated France, in this same National Assembly of hers, has got something, nay something great, momentous, indispensable, cannot be doubted; yet still the question were: Specially what? A question hard to solve, even for calm onlookers at this distance; wholly insoluble to actors in the middle of it. The States-General, created and conflated by the passionate effort of the whole nation, is there as a thing high and lifted up. Hope, jubilating, cries aloud that it will prove a miraculous Brazen Serpent in the Wilderness; whereon whosoever looks, with faith and obedience, shall be healed of all woes and serpent-bites.

We may answer, it will at least prove a symbolic Banner; round which the exasperating complaining Twenty-Five Millions, otherwise isolated and without power, may rally, and work – what it is in them to work. If battle must be the work, as one cannot help expecting, then shall it be a battle-banner (say, an Italian Gonfalon, in its old Republican Carroccio); and shall tower up, car-borne, shining in the wind: and with iron tongue peal forth many a signal. A thing of prime necessity; which whether in the van or in the centre, whether leading or led and driven, must do the fighting multitude incalculable services. For a season, while it floats in the very front, nay as it were stands solitary there, waiting whether force will gather round it, this same National Carroccio, and the signal-peals it rings, are a main object with us.

The omen of the 'slouch-hats clapt on' shows the Commons Deputies to have made up their minds on one thing: that neither Noblesse nor Clergy shall have precedence of them; hardly even Majesty itself. To such length has the Contrat Social, and force of public opinion, carried us. For what is Majesty but the Delegate of the Nation; delegated, and bargained with (even rather tightly), – in some very singular posture of affairs, which Jean Jacques has not fixed the date of?

Coming therefore into their Hall, on the morrow, an inorganic mass of Six Hundred individuals, these Commons Deputies perceive, without terror, that they have it all to themselves. Their Hall is also the Grand or general Hall for all the Three Orders. But the Noblesse and Clergy, it would seem, have retired to their two separate Apartments, or Halls; and are there 'verifying their powers,' not in a conjoint but in a separate capacity. They are to constitute two separate, perhaps separately-voting Orders, then? It is as if both Noblesse and Clergy had silently taken for granted that they already were such! Two Orders against one; and so the Third Order to be left in a perpetual minority?

Much may remain unfixed; but the negative of that is a thing fixed: in the Slouch-hatted heads, in the French Nation's head. Double representation, and all else hitherto gained, were otherwise futile, null. Doubtless, the 'powers must be verified;' – doubtless, the Commission, the electoral Documents of your Deputy must be inspected by his brother Deputies, and found valid: it is the preliminary of all. Neither is this question, of doing it separately or doing it conjointly, a vital one: but if it lead to such? It must be resisted; wise was that maxim, Resist the beginnings! Nay were resistance unadvisable, even dangerous, yet surely pause is very natural: pause, with Twenty-five Millions behind you, may become resistance enough. – The inorganic mass of Commons Deputies will restrict itself to a 'system of inertia,' and for the present remain inorganic.

MERCURY DE BREZE.

Now surely were the time for a 'god from the machine;' there is a nodus worthy of one. The only question is, Which god? Shall it be Mars de Broglie, with his hundred pieces of cannon? – Not yet, answers prudence; so soft, irresolute is King Louis. Let it be Messenger Mercury, our Supreme Usher de Breze.

On the morrow, which is the 20th of June, these Hundred and Forty-nine false Curates, no longer restrainable by his Grace of Paris, will desert in a body: let De Breze intervene, and produce – closed doors! Not only shall there be Royal Session, in that Salle des Menus; but no meeting, nor working (except by carpenters), till then. Your Third Estate, self-styled 'National Assembly,' shall suddenly see itself extruded from its Hall, by carpenters, in this dexterous way; and reduced to do nothing, not even to meet, or articulately lament, – till Majesty, with Seance Royale and new miracles, be ready! In this manner shall De Breze, as Mercury ex machina, intervene; and, if the Oeil-de-Boeuf mistake not, work deliverance from the nodus.

Of poor De Breze we can remark that he has yet prospered in none of his dealings with these Commons. Five weeks ago, when they kissed the hand of Majesty, the mode he took got nothing but censure; and then his 'sincere attachment,' how was it scornfully whiffed aside! Before supper, this night, he writes to President Bailly, a new Letter, to be delivered shortly after dawn tomorrow, in the King's name. Which Letter, however, Bailly in the pride of office, will merely crush together into his pocket, like a bill he does not mean to pay.

Accordingly on Saturday morning the 20th of June, shrill-sounding heralds proclaim through the streets of Versailles, that there is to be a Seance Royale next Monday; and no meeting of the States-General till then. And yet, we observe, President Bailly in sound of this, and with De Breze's Letter in his pocket, is proceeding, with National Assembly at his heels, to the accustomed Salles des Menus; as if De Breze and heralds were mere wind. It is shut, this Salle; occupied by Gardes Francaises. "Where is your Captain?" The Captain shows his royal order: workmen, he is grieved to say, are all busy setting up the platform for his Majesty's Seance; most unfortunately, no admission; admission, at furthest, for President and Secretaries to bring away papers, which the joiners might destroy! – President Bailly enters with Secretaries; and returns bearing papers: alas, within doors, instead of patriotic eloquence, there is now no noise but hammering, sawing, and operative screeching and rumbling! A profanation without parallel.

The Deputies stand grouped on the Paris Road, on this umbrageous Avenue de Versailles; complaining aloud of the indignity done them. Courtiers, it is supposed, look from their windows, and giggle. The morning is none of the comfortablest: raw; it is even drizzling a little. But all travellers pause; patriot gallery-men, miscellaneous spectators increase the groups. Wild counsels alternate. Some desperate Deputies propose to go and hold session on the great outer Staircase at Marly, under the King's windows; for his Majesty, it seems, has driven over thither. Others talk of making the Chateau Forecourt, what they call Place d'Armes, a Runnymede and new Champ de Mai of free Frenchmen: nay of awakening, to sounds of indignant

Patriotism, the echoes of the Oeil-de-boeuf itself. – Notice is given that President Bailly, aided by judicious Guillotin and others, has found place in the Tennis-Court of the Rue St. Francois. Thither, in long-drawn files, hoarse-jingling, like cranes on wing, the Commons Deputies angrily wend.

Strange sight was this in the Rue St. Francois, Vieux Versailles! A naked Tennis-Court, as the pictures of that time still give it: four walls; naked, except aloft some poor wooden penthouse, or roofed spectators'-gallery, hanging round them: – on the floor not now an idle teeheeing, a snapping of balls and rackets; but the bellowing din of an indignant National Representation, scandalously exiled hither! However, a cloud of witnesses looks down on them, from wooden penthouse, from wall-top, from adjoining roof and chimney; rolls towards them from all quarters, with passionate spoken blessings. Some table can be procured to write on; some chair, if not to sit on, then to stand on. The Secretaries undo their tapes; Bailly has constituted the Assembly.

Experienced Mounier, not wholly new to such things, in Parlementary revolts, which he has seen or heard of, thinks that it were well, in these lamentable threatening circumstances, to unite themselves by an Oath. – Universal acclamation, as from smouldering bosoms getting vent! The Oath is redacted; pronounced aloud by President Bailly, – and indeed in such a sonorous tone, that the cloud of witnesses, even outdoors, hear it, and bellow response to it. Six hundred right-hands rise with President Bailly's, to take God above to witness that they will not separate for man below, but will meet in all places, under all circumstances, wheresoever two or three can get together, till they have made the Constitution. Made the Constitution, Friends! That is a long task. Six hundred hands, meanwhile, will sign as they have sworn: six hundred save one; one Loyalist Abdiel, still visible by this sole light-point, and nameable, poor 'M. Martin d'Auch, from Castelnaudary, in Languedoc.' Him they permit to sign or signify refusal; they even save him from the cloud of witnesses, by declaring 'his head deranged.' At four o'clock, the signatures are all appended; new meeting is fixed for Monday morning, earlier than the hour of the Royal Session; that our Hundred and Forty-nine Clerical deserters be not balked: we shall meet 'at the Recollets Church or elsewhere,' in hope that our Hundred and Forty-nine will join us; – and now it is time to go to dinner.

This, then, is the Session of the Tennis-Court, famed Seance du Jeu de Paume; the fame of which has gone forth to all lands. This is Mercurius de Breze's appearance as Deus ex machina; this is the fruit it brings! The giggle of Courtiers in the Versailles Avenue has already died into gaunt silence. Did the distracted Court, with Gardes-des-Sceaux Barentin, Triumvirate and Company, imagine that they could scatter six hundred National Deputies, big with a National Constitution, like as much barndoor poultry, big with next to nothing, – by the white or black rod of a Supreme Usher? Barndoor poultry fly cackling: but National Deputies turn round, lion-faced; and, with uplifted right-hand, swear an Oath that makes the four corners of France tremble.

BROGLIE THE WAR-GOD.

The Court feels indignant that it is conquered; but what then? Another time it will do better. Mercury descended in vain; now has the time come for Mars. – The gods of the Oeil-de-Boeuf have withdrawn into the darkness of their cloudy Ida; and sit there, shaping and forging what may be needful, be it 'billets of a new National Bank,' munitions of war, or things forever inscrutable to men.

Accordingly, what means this 'apparatus of troops'? The National Assembly can get no furtherance for its Committee of Subsistences; can hear only that, at Paris, the Bakers' shops are besieged; that, in the Provinces, people are living on 'meal-husks and boiled grass.' But on all highways there hover dust-clouds, with the march of regiments, with the trailing of cannon: foreign Pandours, of fierce aspect; Salis-Samade, Esterhazy, Royal-Allemand; so many of them foreign, to the number of thirty thousand, – which fear can magnify to fifty: all wending towards Paris and Versailles! Already, on the heights of Montmartre, is a digging and delving; too like a scarping and trenching. The effluence of Paris is arrested Versailles-ward by a barrier of cannon at Sevres Bridge. From the Queen's Mews, cannon stand pointed on the National Assembly Hall itself. The National Assembly has its very slumbers broken by the tramp of soldiery, swarming and defiling, endless, or seemingly endless, all round those spaces, at dead of night, 'without drum-music, without audible word of command.' What means it?

Shall eight, or even shall twelve Deputies, our Mirabeaus, Barnaves at the head of them, be whirled suddenly to the Castle of Ham; the rest ignominiously dispersed to the winds? No National Assembly can make the Constitution with cannon levelled on it from the Queen's Mews! What means this reticence of the Oeil-de-Boeuf, broken only by nods and shrugs? In the mystery of that cloudy Ida, what is it that they forge and shape? – Such questions must distracted Patriotism keep asking, and receive no answer but an echo.

Enough of themselves! But now, above all, while the hungry food-year, which runs from August to August, is getting older; becoming more and more a famine-year? With 'meal-husks and boiled grass,' Brigands may actually collect; and, in crowds, at farm and mansion, howl angrily, Food! Food! It is in vain to send soldiers against them: at sight of soldiers they disperse, they vanish as under ground; then directly reassemble elsewhere for new tumult and plunder. Frightful enough to look upon; but what to hear of, reverberated through Twenty-five Millions of suspicious minds! Brigands and Broglie, open Conflagration, preternatural Rumour are driving mad most hearts in France. What will the issue of these things be?

Good is grapeshot, Messeigneurs, on one condition: that the shooter also were made of metal! But unfortunately he is made of flesh; under his buffs and bandoleers your hired shooter has instincts, feelings, even a kind of thought. It is his kindred, bone of his bone, this same canaille that shall be whiffed; he has brothers in it, a father and mother, – living on meal-husks and boiled grass. His very doxy, not yet 'dead i' the spital,' drives him into military heterodoxy; declares that if he shed Patriot blood, he shall be accursed among men. The soldier, who has seen his pay stolen by rapacious Foulons, his blood wasted by Soubises, Pompadours, and the gates of promotion shut inexorably on him if he were not born noble, – is himself not without griefs against you. Your cause is not the soldier's cause; but, as would seem, your own only, and no other god's nor man's.

TO ARMS!

So hangs it, dubious, fateful, in the sultry days of July. It is the passionate printed advice of M. Marat, to abstain, of all things, from violence. Nevertheless the hungry poor are already burning Town Barriers, where Tribute on eatables is levied; getting clamorous for food.

The twelfth July morning is Sunday; the streets are all placarded with an enormous-sized De par le Roi, 'inviting peaceable citizens to remain within doors,' to feel no alarm, to gather in no crowd. Why so? What mean these 'placards of enormous size'? Above all, what means this clatter of military; dragoons, hussars, rattling in from all points of the compass towards the Place Louis Quinze; with a staid gravity of face, though saluted with mere nicknames, hootings and even missiles? Besenval is with them. Swiss Guards of his are already in the Champs Elysees, with four pieces of artillery.

Have the destroyers descended on us, then? From the Bridge of Sevres to utmost Vincennes, from Saint-Denis to the Champ-de-Mars, we are begirt! Alarm, of the vague unknown, is in every heart. The Palais Royal has become a place of awestruck interjections, silent shakings of the head: one can fancy with what dolorous sound the noon-tide cannon (which the Sun fires at the crossing of his meridian) went off there; bodeful, like an inarticulate voice of doom. Are these troops verily come out 'against Brigands'? Where are the Brigands? What mystery is in the wind? – Hark! a human voice reporting articulately the Job's-news: Necker, People's Minister, Saviour of France, is dismissed. Impossible; incredible! Treasonous to the public peace! Such a voice ought to be choked in the water-works; – had not the news-bringer quickly fled. Nevertheless, friends, make of it what you will, the news is true. Necker is gone. Necker hies northward incessantly, in obedient secrecy, since yesternight. We have a new Ministry: Broglie the War-god; Aristocrat Breteuil; Foulon who said the people might eat grass!

Rumour, therefore, shall arise; in the Palais Royal, and in broad France. Paleness sits on every face; confused tremor and fremescence; waxing into thunder-peals, of Fury stirred on by Fear.

But see Camille Desmoulins, from the Cafe de Foy, rushing out, sibylline in face; his hair streaming, in each hand a pistol! He springs to a table: the Police satellites are eyeing him; alive they shall not take him, not they alive him alive. This time he speaks without stammering: – Friends, shall we die like hunted hares? Like sheep hounded into their pinfold; bleating for mercy, where is no mercy, but only a whetted knife? The hour is come; the supreme hour of Frenchman and Man; when Oppressors are to try conclusions with Oppressed; and the word is, swift Death, or Deliverance forever. Let such hour be well-come! Us, meseems, one cry only befits: To Arms! Let universal Paris, universal France, as with the throat of the whirlwind, sound only: To arms! – "To arms!" yell responsive the innumerable voices: like one great voice, as of a Demon yelling from the air: for all faces wax fire-eyed, all hearts burn up into madness. In such, or fitter words, does Camille evoke the Elemental Powers, in this great moment. – Friends, continues Camille, some rallying sign! Cockades; green ones; – the colour of hope! – As with the flight of locusts, these green tree leaves; green ribands from the neighbouring shops; all green things are snatched, and made cockades of. Camille descends from his table, 'stifled with embraces, wetted with tears;' has a bit of green riband handed him; sticks it in his hat. And now to Curtius' Image-shop there; to the Boulevards; to the four winds; and rest not till France be on fire!

In this manner march they, a mixed, continually increasing multitude; armed with axes, staves and miscellanea; grim, many-sounding, through the streets. Be all Theatres shut; let all dancing, on planked floor, or on the natural greensward, cease! Instead of a Christian Sabbath, and feast of guinguette tabernacles, it shall be a Sorcerer's Sabbath; and Paris, gone rabid, dance, – with the Fiend for piper!

GIVE US ARMS.

On Monday the huge City has awoke, not to its week-day industry: to what a different one! The working man has become a fighting man; has one want only: that of arms. The industry of all crafts has paused; – except it be the smith's, fiercely hammering pikes; and, in a faint degree, the kitchener's, cooking off-hand victuals; for bouche va toujours. Women too are sewing cockades; – not now of green, which being D'Artois colour, the Hotel-de-Ville has had to interfere in it; but of red and blue, our old Paris colours: these, once based on a ground of constitutional white, are the famed TRICOLOR, – which (if Prophecy err not) 'will go round the world.'

All shops, unless it be the Bakers' and Vintners', are shut: Paris is in the streets; – rushing, foaming like some Venice wine-glass into which you had dropped poison. The tocsin, by order, is pealing madly from all steeples. Arms, ye Elector Municipals; thou Flesselles with thy Echevins, give us arms! Flesselles gives what he can: fallacious, perhaps insidious promises of arms from Charleville; order to seek arms here, order to seek them there. The new Municipals give what they can; some three hundred and sixty indifferent firelocks, the equipment of the City-Watch: 'a man in wooden shoes, and without coat, directly clutches one of them, and mounts guard.' Also as hinted, an order to all Smiths to make pikes with their whole soul.

Our Parisian Militia, – which some think it were better to name National Guard, – is prospering as heart could wish. It promised to be forty-eight thousand; but will in few hours double and quadruple that number: invincible, if we had only arms!

But see, the promised Charleville Boxes, marked Artillerie! Here, then, are arms enough? – Conceive the blank face of Patriotism, when it found them filled with rags, foul linen, candle-ends, and bits of wood! Provost of the Merchants, how is this? Neither at the Chartreux Convent, whither we were sent with signed order, is there or ever was there any weapon of war. Nay here, in this Seine Boat, safe under tarpaulins (had not the nose of Patriotism been of the finest), are 'five thousand-weight of gunpowder;' not coming in, but surreptitiously going out! What meanest thou, Flesselles? 'Tis a ticklish game, that of 'amusing' us. Cat plays with captive mouse: but mouse with enraged cat, with enraged National Tiger?

Meanwhile, the faster, O ye black-aproned Smiths, smite; with strong arm and willing heart. This man and that, all stroke from head to heel, shall thunder alternating, and ply the great forge-hammer, till stithy reel and ring again; while ever and anon, overhead, booms the alarm-cannon, – for the City has now got gunpowder. Pikes are fabricated; fifty thousand of them, in six-and-thirty hours: judge whether the Black-aproned have been idle. Dig trenches, unpave the streets, ye others, assiduous, man and maid; cram the earth in barrel-barricades, at each of them a volunteer sentry; pile the whinstones in window-sills and upper rooms. Have scalding pitch, at least boiling water ready, ye weak old women, to pour it and dash it on Royal-Allemand, with your old skinny arms: your shrill curses along with it will not be wanting! – Patrols of the newborn National Guard, bearing torches, scour the streets, all that night; which otherwise are vacant, yet illuminated in every window by order. Strange-looking; like some naphtha-lighted City of the Dead, with here and there a flight of perturbed Ghosts.

O poor mortals, how ye make this Earth bitter for each other; this fearful and wonderful Life fearful and horrible; and Satan has his place in all hearts! Such agonies and ragings and wailings ye have, and have had, in all times: – to be buried all, in so deep silence; and the salt sea is not swoln with your tears.

Great meanwhile is the moment, when tidings of Freedom reach us; when the long-enthralled soul, from amid its chains and squalid stagnancy, arises, were it still only in blindness and bewilderment, and swears by Him that made it, that it will be free! Free? Understand that well, it is the deep commandment, dimmer or clearer, of our whole being, to be free. Freedom is the one purport, wisely aimed at, or unwisely, of all man's struggles, toilings and sufferings, in this Earth. Yes, supreme is such a moment (if thou have known it): first vision as of a flame-girt Sinai, in this our waste Pilgrimage, – which thenceforth wants not its pillar of cloud by day, and pillar of fire by night! Something it is even, – nay, something considerable, when the chains have grown corrosive, poisonous, to be free 'from oppression by our fellow-man.' Forward, ye maddened sons of France; be it towards this destiny or towards that! Around you is but starvation, falsehood, corruption and the clam of death. Where ye are is no abiding.

STORM AND VICTORY.

But, to the living and the struggling, a new, Fourteenth morning dawns. Under all roofs of this distracted City, is the nodus of a drama, not untragical, crowding towards solution. The bustlings and preparings, the tremors and menaces; the tears that fell from old eyes! This day, my sons, ye shall quit you like men. By the memory of your fathers' wrongs, by the hope of your children's rights! Tyranny impends in red wrath: help for you is none if not in your own right hands. This day ye must do or die.

All morning, since nine, there has been a cry everywhere: To the Bastille! Repeated 'deputations of citizens' have been here, passionate for arms; whom de Launay has got dismissed by soft speeches through portholes. Towards noon, Elector Thuriot de la Rosiere gains admittance; finds de Launay indisposed for surrender; nay disposed for blowing up the place rather. Thuriot mounts with him to the battlements: heaps of paving-stones, old iron and missiles lie piled; cannon all duly levelled; in every embrasure a cannon, – only drawn back a little! But outwards behold, O Thuriot, how the multitude flows on, welling through every street; tocsin furiously pealing, all drums beating the generale: the Suburb Saint-Antoine rolling hitherward wholly, as one man! Such vision (spectral yet real) thou, O Thuriot, as from thy Mount of Vision, beholdest in this moment: prophetic of what other Phantasmagories, and loud-gibbering Spectral Realities, which, thou yet beholdest not, but shalt! "Que voulez vous?" said de Launay, turning pale at the sight, with an air of reproach, almost of menace. "Monsieur," said Thuriot, rising into the moral-sublime, "What mean you? Consider if I could not precipitate both of us from this height," – say only a hundred feet, exclusive of the walled ditch! Whereupon de Launay fell silent. Thuriot shews himself from some pinnacle, to comfort the multitude becoming suspicious, fremescent: then descends; departs with protest; with warning addressed also to the Invalides, – on whom, however, it produces but a mixed indistinct impression. The old heads are none of the clearest; besides, it is said, de Launay has been profuse of beverages (prodigua des buissons). They think, they will not fire, – if not fired on, if they can help it; but must, on the whole, be ruled considerably by circumstances.

Wo to thee, de Launay, in such an hour, if thou canst not, taking some one firm decision, rule circumstances! Soft speeches will not serve; hard grape-shot is questionable; but hovering between the two is unquestionable. Ever wilder swells the tide of men; their infinite hum waxing ever louder, into imprecations, perhaps into crackle of stray musketry, – which latter, on walls nine feet thick, cannot do execution. The Outer Drawbridge has been lowered for Thuriot; new deputation of citizens (it is the third, and noisiest of all) penetrates that way into the Outer Court: soft speeches producing no clearance of these, de Launay gives fire; pulls up his Drawbridge. A slight sputter; – which has kindled the too combustible chaos; made it a roaring fire-chaos! Bursts forth insurrection, at sight of its own blood (for there were deaths by that sputter of fire), into endless rolling explosion of musketry, distraction, execration; – and overhead, from the Fortress, let one great gun, with its grape-shot, go booming, to shew what we could do. The Bastille is besieged!

On, then, all Frenchmen that have hearts in their bodies! Roar with all your throats, of cartilage and metal, ye Sons of Liberty; stir spasmodically whatsoever of utmost faculty is in you, soul, body or spirit; for it is the hour! Smite, thou Louis Tournay, cartwright of the Marais, old-soldier of the Regiment Dauphine; smite at that Outer Drawbridge chain, though the fiery hail whistles round thee! Never, over nave or felloe, did thy axe strike such a stroke. Down with it, man; down with it to Orcus: let the whole accursed Edifice sink thither, and Tyranny be swallowed up for ever! Mounted, some say on the roof of the guard-room, some 'on bayonets stuck into joints of the wall,' Louis Tournay smites, brave Aubin Bonnemere (also an old soldier) seconding him: the chain yields, breaks; the huge Drawbridge slams down, thundering (avec fracas). Glorious: and yet, alas, it is still but the outworks. The Eight grim Towers, with their Invalides' musketry, their paving stones and cannon-mouths, still soar aloft intact; – Ditch yawning impassable, stone-faced; the inner Drawbridge with its back towards us: the Bastille is still to take!

To describe this Siege of the Bastille (thought to be one of the most important in history) perhaps transcends the talent of mortals. Could one but, after infinite reading, get to understand so much as the plan of the building! But there is open Esplanade, at the end of the Rue Saint-Antoine; there are such Forecourts, Cour Avance, Cour de l'Orme, arched Gateway (where Louis Tournay now fights); then new drawbridges, dormant-bridges, rampart-bastions, and the grim Eight Towers: a labyrinthic Mass, high-frowning there, of all ages from twenty years to four hundred and twenty; – beleaguered, in this its last hour, as we said, by mere Chaos come again! Ordnance of all calibres; throats of all capacities; men of all plans, every man his own engineer: seldom since the war of Pygmies and Cranes was there seen so anomalous a thing. Half-pay Elie is home for a suit of regimentals; no one would heed him in coloured clothes: half-pay Hulin is haranguing Gardes Francaises in the Place de Greve. Frantic Patriots pick up the grape-shots; bear them, still hot (or seemingly so), to the Hotel-de-Ville: – Paris, you perceive, is to be burnt! Flesselles is 'pale to the very lips' for the roar of the multitude grows deep. Paris wholly has got to the acme of its frenzy; whirled, all ways, by panic madness. At every street-barricade, there whirls simmering, a minor whirlpool, – strengthening the barricade, since God knows what is coming; and all minor whirlpools play distractedly into that grand Fire-Mahlstrom which is lashing round the Bastille.

Blood flows, the aliment of new madness. The wounded are carried into houses of the Rue Cerisaie; the dying leave their last mandate not to yield till the accursed Stronghold fall. And yet, alas, how fall? The walls are so thick! Deputations, three in number, arrive from the Hotel-de-Ville; Abbe Fouchet (who was of one) can say, with what almost superhuman courage of benevolence. These wave their Town-flag in the arched Gateway; and stand, rolling their drum; but to no purpose. In such Crack of Doom, de Launay cannot hear them, dare not believe them: they return, with justified rage, the whew of lead still singing in their ears. What to do? The Firemen are here, squirting with their fire-pumps on the Invalides' cannon, to wet the touchholes; they unfortunately cannot squirt so high; but produce only clouds of spray. Individuals of classical knowledge propose catapults. Santerre, the sonorous Brewer of the Suburb Saint-Antoine, advises rather that the place be fired, by a 'mixture of phosphorous and oil-of-turpentine spouted up through forcing pumps:' O Spinola-Santerre, hast thou the mixture ready? Every man his own engineer! And still the fire-deluge abates not; even women are firing, and Turks; at least one woman (with her sweetheart), and one Turk. Gardes Francaises have come: real cannon, real cannoneers. Usher Maillard is busy; half-pay Elie, half-pay Hulin rage in the midst of thousands.

How the great Bastille Clock ticks (inaudible) in its Inner Court there, at its ease, hour after hour; as if nothing special, for it or the world, were passing! It tolled One when the firing began; and is now pointing towards Five, and still the firing slakes not. – Far down, in their vaults, the seven Prisoners hear muffled din as of earthquakes; their Turnkeys answer vaguely.

Wo to thee, de Launay, with thy poor hundred Invalides!

Broglie is distant, and his ears heavy: Besenval hears, but can send no help. One poor troop of Hussars has crept, reconnoitring, cautiously along the Quais, as far as the Pont Neuf. "We are come to join you," said the Captain; for the crowd seems shoreless. A large-headed dwarfish individual, of smoke-bleared aspect, shambles forward, opening his blue lips, for there is sense in him; and croaks: "Alight then, and give up your arms!" the Hussar-Captain is too happy to be escorted to the Barriers, and dismissed on parole. Who the squat individual was? Men answer, it is M. Marat, author of the excellent pacific Avis au Peuple! Great truly, O thou remarkable Dogleech, is this thy day of emergence and new birth: and yet this same day come four years – ! – But let the curtains of the future hang.

What shall de Launay do? One thing only de Launay could have done: what he said he would do. Fancy him sitting, from the first, with lighted taper, within arm's length of the Powder-Magazine; motionless, like old Roman Senator, or bronze Lamp-holder; coldly apprising Thuriot, and all men, by a slight motion of his eye, what his resolution was: – Harmless he sat there, while unharmed; but the King's Fortress, meanwhile, could, might, would, or should, in nowise, be surrendered, save to the King's Messenger: one old man's life worthless, so it be lost with honour; but think, ye brawling canaille, how will it be when a whole Bastille springs skyward! – In such statuesque, taper-holding attitude, one fancies de Launay might have left Thuriot, the red Clerks of the Bazoche, Cure of Saint-Stephen and all the tagrag-and-bobtail of the world, to work their will.

And yet, withal, he could not do it. Hast thou considered how each man's heart is so tremulously responsive to the hearts of all men; hast thou noted how omnipotent is the very sound of many men? How their shriek of indignation palsies the strong soul; their howl of contumely withers with unfelt pangs? The Ritter Gluck confessed that the ground-tone of the noblest passage, in one of his noblest Operas, was the voice of the Populace he had heard at Vienna, crying to their Kaiser: Bread! Bread! Great is the combined voice of men; the utterance of their instincts, which are truer than their thoughts: it is the greatest a man encounters, among the sounds and shadows, which make up this World of Time. He who can resist that, has his footing some where beyond Time. De Launay could not do it. Distracted, he hovers between the two; hopes in the middle of despair; surrenders not his Fortress; declares that he will blow it up, seizes torches to blow it up, and does not blow it. Unhappy old de Launay, it is the death-agony of thy Bastille and thee! Jail, Jailoring and Jailor, all three, such as they may have been, must finish.

For four hours now has the World-Bedlam roared: call it the World-Chimaera, blowing fire! The poor Invalides have sunk under their battlements, or rise only with reversed muskets: they have made a white flag of napkins; go beating the chamade, or seeming to beat, for one can hear nothing. The very Swiss at the Portcullis look weary of firing; disheartened in the fire-deluge: a porthole at the drawbridge is opened, as by one that would speak. See Huissier Maillard, the shifty man! On his plank, swinging over the abyss of that stone-Ditch; plank resting on parapet, balanced by weight of Patriots, – he hovers perilous: such a Dove towards such an Ark! Deftly, thou shifty Usher: one man already fell; and lies smashed, far down there, against the masonry! Usher

Maillard falls not: deftly, unerring he walks, with outspread palm. The Swiss holds a paper through his porthole; the shifty Usher snatches it, and returns. Terms of surrender: Pardon, immunity to all! Are they accepted? – "Foi d'officier, On the word of an officer," answers half-pay Hulin, – or half-pay Elie, for men do not agree on it, "they are!" Sinks the drawbridge, – Usher Maillard bolting it when down; rushes-in the living deluge: the Bastille is fallen! Victoire! La Bastille est prise!

MAKE THE CONSTITUTION.

Here perhaps is the place to fix, a little more precisely, what these two words, French Revolution, shall mean; for, strictly considered, they may have as many meanings as there are speakers of them. All things are in revolution; in change from moment to moment, which becomes sensible from epoch to epoch: in this Time-World of ours there is properly nothing else but revolution and mutation, and even nothing else conceivable. Revolution, you answer, means speedier change. Whereupon one has still to ask: How speedy? At what degree of speed; in what particular points of this variable course, which varies in velocity, but can never stop till Time itself stops, does revolution begin and end; cease to be ordinary mutation, and again become such? It is a thing that will depend on definition more or less arbitrary.

For ourselves we answer that French Revolution means here the open violent Rebellion, and Victory, of disimprisoned Anarchy against corrupt worn-out Authority: how Anarchy breaks prison; bursts up from the infinite Deep, and rages uncontrollable, immeasurable, enveloping a world; in phasis after phasis of fever-frenzy; – 'till the frenzy burning itself out, and what elements of new Order it held (since all Force holds such) developing themselves, the Uncontrollable be got, if not reimprisoned, yet harnessed, and its mad forces made to work towards their object as sane regulated ones. For as Hierarchies and Dynasties of all kinds, Theocracies, Aristocracies, Autocracies, Strumpetocracies, have ruled over the world; so it was appointed, in the decrees of Providence, that this same Victorious Anarchy, Jacobinism, Sansculottism, French Revolution, Horrors of French Revolution, or what else mortals name it, should have its turn. The 'destructive wrath' of Sansculottism: this is what we speak, having unhappily no voice for singing.

Surely a great Phenomenon: nay it is a transcendental one, overstepping all rules and experience; the crowning Phenomenon of our Modern Time. For here again, most unexpectedly, comes antique Fanaticism in new and newest vesture; miraculous, as all Fanaticism is. Call it the Fanaticism of 'making away with formulas, de humer les formulas.' The world of formulas, the formed regulated world, which all habitable world is, – must needs hate such Fanaticism like death; and be at deadly variance with it. The world of formulas must conquer it; or failing that, must die execrating it, anathematising it; – can nevertheless in nowise prevent its being and its having been. The Anathemas are there, and the miraculous Thing is there.

Whence it cometh? Whither it goeth? These are questions! When the age of Miracles lay faded into the distance as an incredible tradition, and even the age of Conventionalities was now old; and Man's Existence had for long generations rested on mere formulas which were grown hollow by course of time; and it seemed as if no Reality any longer existed but only Phantasms of realities, and God's Universe were the work of the Tailor and Upholsterer mainly, and men were buckram masks that went about becking and grimacing there, – on a sudden, the Earth yawns asunder, and amid Tartarean smoke, and glare of fierce brightness, rises SANSCULOTTISM, many-headed, fire-breathing, and asks: What think ye of me? Well may the buckram masks start together, terror-struck; 'into expressive well-concerted groups!' It is indeed, Friends, a most singular, most fatal thing. Let whosoever is but buckram and a phantasm look to it: ill verily may it fare with him; here methinks he cannot much longer be. Wo also to many a one who is not wholly buckram, but partially real and human! The age of Miracles has come back! 'Behold the World-Phoenix, in fire-consummation and fire-creation; wide are her fanning wings; loud is her death-melody, of battle-thunders and falling towns; skyward lashes the funeral flame, enveloping all things: it is the Death-Birth of a World!'

PART II – THE CONSTITUTION

TO FLY OR NOT TO FLY.

The truth is Royalism sees itself verging towards sad extremities; nearer and nearer daily. From over the Rhine it comes asserted that the King in his Tuileries is not free: this the poor King may contradict, with the official mouth, but in his heart feels often to be undeniable. Civil Constitution of the Clergy; Decree of ejectment against Dissidents from it: not even to this latter, though almost his conscience rebels, can he say 'Nay; but, after two months' hesitating, signs this also. It was on January 21st,' of this 1790, that he signed it; to the sorrow of his poor heart yet, on another Twenty-first of January! Whereby come Dissident ejected Priests; unconquerable Martyrs according to some, incurable chicaning Traitors according to others. And so there has arrived what we once foreshadowed: with Religion, or with the Cant and Echo of Religion, all France is rent asunder in a new rupture of continuity; complicating, embittering all the older; – to be cured only, by stern surgery, in La Vendee!

Unhappy Royalty, unhappy Majesty, Hereditary (Representative), Representant Hereditaire, or however they can name him; of whom much is expected, to whom little is given! Blue National Guards encircle that Tuileries; a Lafayette, thin constitutional Pedant; clear, thin, inflexible, as water, turned to thin ice; whom no Queen's heart can

65

love. National Assembly, its pavilion spread where we know, sits near by, keeping continual hubbub. From without nothing but Nanci Revolts, sack of Castries Hotels, riots and seditions; riots, North and South, at Aix, at Douai, at Befort, Usez, Perpignan, at Nismes, and that incurable Avignon of the Pope's: a continual crackling and sputtering of riots from the whole face of France; – testifying how electric it grows. Add only the hard winter, the famished strikes of operatives; that continual running-bass of Scarcity, ground-tone and basis of all other Discords!

The plan of Royalty, so far as it can be said to have any fixed plan, is still, as ever, that of flying towards the frontiers. In very truth, the only plan of the smallest promise for it! Fly to Bouille; bristle yourself round with cannon, served by your 'forty-thousand undebauched Germans:' summon the National Assembly to follow you, summon what of it is Royalist, Constitutional, gainable by money; dissolve the rest, by grapeshot if need be. Let Jacobinism and Revolt, with one wild wail, fly into Infinite Space; driven by grapeshot. Thunder over France with the cannon's mouth; commanding, not entreating, that this riot cease. And then to rule afterwards with utmost possible Constitutionality; doing justice, loving mercy; being Shepherd of this indigent People, not Shearer merely, and Shepherd's-similitude! All this, if ye dare. If ye dare not, then in Heaven's name go to sleep: other handsome alternative seems none.

Nay, it were perhaps possible; with a man to do it. For if such inexpressible whirlpool of Babylonish confusions (which our Era is) cannot be stilled by man, but only by Time and men, a man may moderate its paroxysms, may balance and sway, and keep himself unswallowed on the top of it, – as several men and Kings in these days do. Much is possible for a man; men will obey a man that kens and cans, and name him reverently their Ken-ning or King. Did not Charlemagne rule? Consider too whether he had smooth times of it; hanging 'thirty-thousand Saxons over the Weser-Bridge,' at one dread swoop! So likewise, who knows but, in this same distracted fanatic France, the right man may verily exist? An olive-complexioned taciturn man; for the present, Lieutenant in the Artillery-service, who once sat studying Mathematics at Brienne? The same who walked in the morning to correct proof-sheets at Dole, and enjoyed a frugal breakfast with M. Joly? Such a one is gone, whither also famed General Paoli his friend is gone, in these very days, to see old scenes in native Corsica, and what Democratic good can be done there.

"You know not the Queen," said Mirabeau once in confidence; "her force of mind is prodigious; she is a man for courage." And so, under the void Night, on the crown of that knoll, she has spoken with a Mirabeau: he has kissed loyally the queenly hand, and said with enthusiasm: "Madame, the Monarchy is saved!" – Possible? The Foreign Powers, mysteriously sounded, gave favourable guarded response; Bouillé is at Metz, and could find forty-thousand sure Germans. With a Mirabeau for head, and a Bouillé for hand, something verily is possible, – if Fate intervene not.

But figure under what thousandfold wrappages, and cloaks of darkness, Royalty, meditating these things, must involve itself. There are men with 'Tickets of Entrance;' there are chivalrous consultings, mysterious plottings. Consider also whether, involve as it like, plotting Royalty can escape the glance of Patriotism; lynx-eyes, by the ten thousand fixed on it, which see in the dark! Patriotism knows much: know the dirks made to order, and can specify the shops; knows Sieur Motier's legions of mouchards; the Tickets of Entree, and men in black; and how plan of evasion succeeds plan, – or may be supposed to succeed it. Then conceive the couplets chanted at the Theatre de Vaudeville; or worse, the whispers, significant nods of traitors in moustaches. Conceive, on the other hand, the loud cry of alarm that came through the Hundred-and-Thirty Journals; the Dionysius'-Ear of each of the Forty-eight Sections, wakeful night and day.

MIRABEAU.

The spirit of France waxes ever more acrid, fever-sick: towards the final outburst of dissolution and delirium. Suspicion rules all minds: contending parties cannot now commingle; stand separated sheer asunder, eying one another, in most aguish mood, of cold terror or hot rage. Counter-Revolution, Days of Poniards, Castries Duels; Flight of Mesdames, of Monsieur and Royalty! Journalism shrills ever louder its cry of alarm. The sleepless Dionysius's Ear of the Forty-eight Sections, how feverishly quick has it grown; convulsing with strange pangs the whole sick Body, as in such sleeplessness and sickness, the ear will do!

Since Royalists get Poniards made to order, and a Sieur Motier is no better than he should be, shall not Patriotism too, even of the indigent sort, have Pikes, secondhand Firelocks, in readiness for the worst? The anvils ring, during this March month, with hammering of Pikes. A Constitutional Municipality promulgated its Placard, that no citizen except the 'active or cash-citizen' was entitled to have arms; but there rose, instantly responsive, such a tempest of astonishment from Club and Section, that the Constitutional Placard, almost next morning, had to cover itself up, and die away into inanity, in a second improved edition. So the hammering continues; as all that it betokens does.

Mark, again, how the extreme tip of the Left is mounting in favour, if not in its own National Hall, yet with the Nation, especially with Paris. For in such universal panic of doubt, the opinion that is sure of itself, as the meagrest opinion may the soonest be, is the one to which all men will rally. Great is Belief, were it never so meagre; and leads captive the doubting heart! Incorruptible Robespierre has been elected Public Accuser in our new Courts of Judicature; virtuous Petion, it is thought, may rise to be Mayor. Cordelier Danton, called also by triumphant majorities, sits at the Departmental Council-table; colleague there of Mirabeau. Of incorruptible Robespierre it was long ago predicted that he might go far, mean meagre mortal though he was; for Doubt dwelt not in him.

Under which circumstances ought not Royalty likewise to cease doubting, and begin deciding and acting? Royalty has always that sure trump-card in its hand: Flight out of Paris. Which sure trump-card, Royalty, as we see, keeps ever and anon clutching at, grasping; and swashes it forth tentatively; yet never tables it, still puts it back again. Play it, O Royalty! If there be a chance left, this seems it, and verily the last chance; and now every hour is rendering this a doubtfuller. Alas, one would so fain both fly and not fly; play one's card and have it to play. Royalty, in all human likelihood, will not play its trump-card till the honours, one after one, be mainly lost; and such trumping of it prove to be the sudden finish of the game!

Here accordingly a question always arises; of the prophetic sort; which cannot now be answered. Suppose Mirabeau, with whom Royalty takes deep counsel, as with a Prime Minister that cannot yet legally avow himself as such, had got his arrangements completed? Arrangements he has; far-stretching plans that dawn fitfully on us, by fragments, in the confused darkness. Thirty Departments ready to sign loyal Addresses, of prescribed tenor: King carried out of Paris, but only to Compiegne and Rouen, hardly to Metz, since, once for all, no Emigrant rabble shall take the lead in it: National Assembly consenting, by dint of loyal Addresses, by management, by force of Bouille, to hear reason, and follow thither! Was it so, on these terms, that Jacobinism and Mirabeau were then to grapple, in their Hercules-and-Typhon duel; death inevitable for the one or the other? The duel itself is determined on, and sure: but on what terms; much more, with what issue, we in vain guess. It is vague darkness all: unknown what is to be; unknown even what has already been. The giant Mirabeau walks in darkness, as we said; companionless, on wild ways: what his thoughts during these months were, no record of Biographer, not vague Fils Adoptif, will now ever disclose.

To us, endeavouring to cast his horoscope, it of course remains doubly vague. There is one Herculean man, in internecine duel with him, there is Monster after Monster. Emigrant Noblesse return, sword on thigh, vaunting of their Loyalty never sullied; descending from the air, like Harpy-swarms with ferocity, with obscene greed. Earthward there is the Typhon of Anarchy, Political, Religious; sprawling hundred-headed, say with Twenty-five million heads; wide as the area of France; fierce as Frenzy; strong in very Hunger. With these shall the Serpent-queller do battle continually, and expect no rest.

As for the King, he as usual will go wavering chameleonlike; changing colour and purpose with the colour of his environment; – good for no Kingly use. On one royal person, on the Queen only, can Mirabeau perhaps place dependance. It is possible, the greatness of this man, not unskilled too in blandishments, courtiership, and graceful adroitness, might, with most legitimate sorcery, fascinate the volatile Queen, and fix her to him. She has courage for all noble daring; an eye and a heart: the soul of Theresa's Daughter. 'Faut il-donc, Is it fated then,' she passionately writes to her Brother, 'that I with the blood I am come of, with the sentiments I have, must live and die among such mortals?' Alas, poor Princess, Yes. 'She is the only man,' as Mirabeau observes, 'whom his Majesty has about him.' Of one other man Mirabeau is still surer: of himself. There lies his resources; sufficient or insufficient.

Dim and great to the eye of Prophecy looks the future! A perpetual life-and-death battle; confusion from above and from below; – mere confused darkness for us; with here and there some streak of faint lurid light. We see King perhaps laid aside; not tonsured, tonsuring is out of fashion now; but say, sent away any whither, with handsome annual allowance, and stock of smith-tools. We see a Queen and Dauphin, Regent and Minor; a Queen 'mounted on horseback,' in the din of battles, with Moriamur pro rege nostro! 'Such a day,' Mirabeau writes, 'may come.'

Din of battles, wars more than civil, confusion from above

71

and from below: in such environment the eye of Prophecy sees Comte de Mirabeau, like some Cardinal de Retz, stormfully maintain himself; with head all-devising, heart all-daring, if not victorious, yet unvanquished, while life is left him. The specialties and issues of it, no eye of Prophecy can guess at: it is clouds, we repeat, and tempestuous night; and in the middle of it, now visible, far darting, now labouring in eclipse, is Mirabeau indomitably struggling to be Cloud-Compeller! – One can say that, had Mirabeau lived, the History of France and of the World had been different. Further, that the man would have needed, as few men ever did, the whole compass of that same 'Art of Daring, Art d'Oser,' which he so prized; and likewise that he, above all men then living, would have practised and manifested it. Finally, that some substantiality, and no empty simulacrum of a formula, would have been the result realised by him: a result you could have loved, a result you could have hated; by no likelihood, a result you could only have rejected with closed lips, and swept into quick forgetfulness for ever. Had Mirabeau lived one other year!

DEATH OF MIRABEAU.

But Mirabeau could not live another year, any more than he could live another thousand years. Men's years are numbered, and the tale of Mirabeau's was now complete. Important, or unimportant; to be mentioned in World-History for some centuries, or not to be mentioned there beyond a day or two, – it matters not to peremptory Fate. From amid the press of ruddy busy Life, the Pale Messenger beckons silently: wide-spreading interests, projects, salvation of French Monarchies, what thing soever man has on hand, he must suddenly quit it all, and go. Wert thou saving French Monarchies; wert thou blacking shoes on the Pont Neuf! The most important of men cannot stay; did the World's History depend on an hour, that hour is not to be given. Whereby, indeed, it comes that these same would-have-beens are mostly a vanity; and the World's History could never in the least be what it would, or might, or should, by any manner of potentiality, but simply and altogether what it is.

The fierce wear and tear of such an existence has wasted out the giant oaken strength of Mirabeau. A fret and fever that keeps heart and brain on fire: excess of effort, of excitement; excess of all kinds: labour incessant, almost beyond credibility! 'If I had not lived with him,' says Dumont, 'I should never have known what a man can make of one day; what things may be placed within the interval of twelve hours. A day for this man was more than a week or a month is for others: the mass of things he guided on together was prodigious; from the scheming to the executing not a moment lost.' "Monsieur le Comte," said his Secretary to him once, "what you require is impossible." – "Impossible!" answered he starting from his chair, "Ne me dites jamais ce bete de mot, Never name to me that blockhead of a word." And then the social repasts; the dinner which he gives as Commandant of National Guards, which 'costs five hundred pounds;' alas, and 'the Sirens of the Opera;' and all the ginger that is hot in the mouth: – down what a course is this man hurled! Cannot Mirabeau stop; cannot he fly, and save himself alive? No! There is a Nessus' Shirt on this Hercules; he must storm and burn there, without rest, till he be consumed. Human strength, never so Herculean, has its measure. Herald shadows flit pale across the fire-brain of Mirabeau; heralds of the pale repose. While he tosses and storms, straining every nerve, in that sea of ambition and confusion, there comes, sombre and still, a monition that for him the issue of it will be swift death.

In January last, you might see him as President of the Assembly; 'his neck wrapt in linen cloths, at the evening session:' there was sick heat of the blood, alternate darkening and flashing in the eye-sight; he had to apply leeches, after the morning labour, and preside bandaged. 'At parting he embraced me,' says Dumont, 'with an emotion I had never seen in him: "I am dying, my friend; dying as by slow fire; we shall perhaps not meet again. When I am gone, they will know what the value of me was. The miseries I have held back will burst from all sides on France."' Sickness gives louder warning; but cannot be listened to. On the 27th day of March, proceeding towards the Assembly, he had to seek rest and help in Friend de Lamarck's, by the road; and lay there, for an hour, half-fainted, stretched on a sofa. To the Assembly nevertheless he went, as if in spite of Destiny itself; spoke, loud and eager, five several times; then quitted the Tribune – for ever. He steps out, utterly exhausted, into the Tuileries Gardens; many people press round him, as usual, with applications, memorials; he says to the Friend who was with him: Take me out of this!

And so, on the last day of March 1791, endless anxious multitudes beset the Rue de la Chaussee d'Antin; incessantly inquiring: within doors there, in that House numbered in our time '42,' the over wearied giant has fallen down, to die. Crowds, of all parties and kinds; of all ranks from the King to the meanest man! The King sends publicly twice a-day to inquire; privately besides: from the world at large there is no end of inquiring. 'A written bulletin is handed out every three hours,' is copied and circulated; in the end, it is printed. The People spontaneously keep silence; no carriage shall enter with its noise: there is crowding pressure; but the Sister of Mirabeau is reverently recognised, and has free way made for her. The People stand mute, heart-stricken; to all it seems as if a great calamity were nigh: as if the last man of France, who could have swayed these coming troubles, lay there at hand-grips with the unearthly Power.

The silence of a whole People, the wakeful toil of Cabanis, Friend and Physician, skills not: on Saturday, the second day of April, Mirabeau feels that the last of the Days has risen for him; that, on this day, he has to depart and be no more. His death is Titanic, as his life has been. Lit up, for the last time, in the glare of coming dissolution, the mind of the man is all glowing and burning; utters itself in sayings, such as men long remember. He longs to live, yet acquiesces in death, argues not with the inexorable. His speech is wild and wondrous: unearthly Phantasms dancing now their torch-dance round his soul; the soul itself looking out, fire-radiant, motionless, girt together for that great hour! At times comes a beam of light from him on the world he is quitting. "I carry in my heart the death-dirge of the French Monarchy; the dead remains of it will now be the spoil of the factious." Or again, when he heard the cannon fire, what is characteristic too: "Have we the Achilles' Funeral already?" So likewise, while some friend is supporting him: "Yes, support that head; would I could bequeath it thee!" For the man dies as he has lived; self-conscious, conscious of a world looking on. He gazes forth on the young Spring, which for him will never be Summer. The Sun has risen; he says: "Si ce n'est pas la Dieu, c'est du moins son cousin germain." Death has mastered the outworks; power of speech is gone; the citadel of the heart still holding out: the moribund giant, passionately, by sign, demands paper and pen; writes his passionate demand for opium, to end these agonies. The sorrowful Doctor shakes his head: Dormir 'To sleep,' writes the other, passionately pointing at it! So dies a gigantic Heathen and Titan; stumbling blindly, undismayed, down to his rest. At half-past eight in the morning, Dr. Petit, standing at the foot of the bed, says "Il ne souffre plus." His suffering and his working are now ended.

GRANDE ACCEPTATION.

In the last nights of September, when the autumnal equinox is past, and grey September fades into brown October, why are the Champs Elysees illuminated; why is Paris dancing, and flinging fire-works? They are gala-nights, these last of September; Paris may well dance, and the Universe: the Edifice of the Constitution is completed! Completed; nay revised, to see that there was nothing insufficient in it; solemnly proferred to his Majesty; solemnly accepted by him, to the sound of cannon-salvoes, on the fourteenth of the month. And now by such illumination, jubilee, dancing and fire-working, do we joyously handsel the new Social Edifice, and first raise heat and reek there, in the name of Hope.

It is the last afternoon of September, 1791; on the morrow morning the new Legislative will begin.

So, amid glitter of illuminated streets and Champs Elysees, and crackle of fireworks and glad deray, has the first National Assembly vanished; dissolving, as they well say, into blank Time; and is no more. National Assembly is gone, its work remaining; as all Bodies of men go, and as man himself goes: it had its beginning, and must likewise have its end. A Phantasm-Reality born of Time, as the rest of us are; flitting ever backwards now on the tide of Time: to be long remembered of men. Very strange Assemblages, Sanhedrims, Amphictyonics, Trades Unions, Ecumenic Councils, Parliaments and Congresses, have met together on this Planet, and dispersed again; but a stranger Assemblage than this august Constituent, or with a stranger mission, perhaps never met there. Seen from the distance, this also will be a miracle. Twelve Hundred human individuals, with the Gospel of Jean-Jacques Rousseau in their pocket, congregating in the name of Twenty-five Millions, with full assurance of faith, to 'make the Constitution:' such sight, the acme and main product of the Eighteenth Century, our World can witness once only. For Time is rich in wonders, in monstrosities most rich; and is observed never to repeat himself, or any of his Gospels: – surely least of all, this Gospel according to Jean-Jacques. Once it was right and indispensable, since such had become the Belief of men; but once also is enough.

They have made the Constitution, these Twelve Hundred Jean-Jacques Evangelists; not without result. Near twenty-nine months they sat, with various fortune; in various capacity; – always, we may say, in that capacity of carborne Caroccio, and miraculous Standard of the Revolt of Men, as a Thing high and lifted up; whereon whosoever looked might hope healing. They have seen much: cannons levelled on them; then suddenly, by interposition of the Powers, the cannons drawn back; and a war-god Broglie vanishing, in thunder not his own, amid the dust and downrushing of a Bastille and Old Feudal France. They have suffered somewhat: Royal Session, with rain and Oath of the Tennis-Court; Nights of Pentecost; Insurrections of Women. Also have they not done somewhat? Made the Constitution, and managed all things the while; passed, in these twenty-nine months, 'twenty-five hundred Decrees,' which on the average is some three for each day, including Sundays! Brevity, one finds, is possible, at times: had not Moreau de St. Mery to give three thousand orders before rising from his seat? – There was valour (or value) in these men; and a kind of faith, – were it only faith in this, That cobwebs are not cloth; that a Constitution could be made. Cobwebs and chimeras ought verily to disappear; for a Reality there is. Let formulas, soul-killing, and now grown body-killing, insupportable, begone, in the name of Heaven and Earth! – Time, as we say, brought forth these Twelve Hundred; Eternity was before them, Eternity behind: they worked, as we all do, in the confluence of Two Eternities; what work was given them. Say not that it was nothing they did. Consciously they did somewhat; unconsciously how much! They had their giants and their dwarfs, they accomplished their good and their evil; they are gone, and return no more. Shall they not go with our blessing, in these circumstances; with our mild farewell?

By post, by diligence, on saddle or sole; they are gone: towards the four winds! Not a few over the marches, to rank at Coblentz. Thither wended Maury, among others; but in the end towards Rome, – to be clothed there in red Cardinal plush; in falsehood as in a garment; pet son (her last-born?)

of the Scarlet Woman. Talleyrand-Perigord, excommunicated Constitutional Bishop, will make his way to London; to be Ambassador, spite of the Self-denying Law; brisk young Marquis Chauvelin acting as Ambassador's-Cloak. In London too, one finds Petion the virtuous; harangued and haranguing, pledging the wine-cup with Constitutional Reform Clubs, in solemn tavern-dinner. Incorruptible Robespierre retires for a little to native Arras: seven short weeks of quiet; the last appointed him in this world. Public Accuser in the Paris Department, acknowledged highpriest of the Jacobins; the glass of incorruptible thin Patriotism, for his narrow emphasis is loved of all the narrow, – this man seems to be rising, somewhither? He sells his small heritage at Arras; accompanied by a Brother and a Sister, he returns, scheming out with resolute timidity a small sure destiny for himself and them, to his old lodging, at the Cabinet-maker's, in the Rue St. Honore: – O resolute-tremulous incorruptible seagreen man, towards what a destiny!

Lafayette, for his part, will lay down the command. He retires Cincinnatus-like to his hearth and farm; but soon leaves them again. Our National Guard, however, shall henceforth have no one Commandant; but all Colonels shall command in succession, month about. Other Deputies we have met, or Dame de Stael has met, 'sauntering in a thoughtful manner;' perhaps uncertain what to do. Some, as Barnave, the Lameths, and their Duport, will continue here in Paris: watching the new biennial Legislative, Parliament the First; teaching it to walk, if so might be; and the Court to lead it.

Thus these: sauntering in a thoughtful manner; travelling by post or diligence, – whither Fate beckons. Giant Mirabeau slumbers in the Pantheon of Great Men: and France? and Europe? – The brass-lunged Hawkers sing "Grand Acceptation, Monarchic Constitution" through these gay crowds: the Morrow, grandson of Yesterday, must be what it can, as To-day its father is. Our new biennial Legislative begins to constitute itself on the first of October, 1791.

KINGS AND EMIGRANTS.

Extremely rheumatic Constitutions have been known to march, and keep on their feet, though in a staggering sprawling manner, for long periods, in virtue of one thing only: that the Head were healthy. But this Head of the French Constitution! What King Louis is and cannot help being, Readers already know. A King who cannot take the Constitution, nor reject the Constitution: nor do anything at all, but miserably ask, What shall I do? A King environed with endless confusions; in whose own mind is no germ of order. Haughty implacable remnants of Noblesse struggling with humiliated repentant Barnave-Lameths: struggling in that obscure element of fetchers and carriers, of Half-pay braggarts from the Cafe Valois, of Chambermaids, whisperers, and subaltern officious persons; fierce Patriotism looking on all the while, more and more suspicious, from without: what, in such struggle, can they do? At best, cancel one another, and produce zero. Poor King! Barnave and your Senatorial Jaucourts speak earnestly into this ear; Bertrand-Moleville, and Messengers from Coblentz, speak earnestly into that: the poor Royal head turns to the one side and to the other side; can turn itself fixedly to no side. Let Decency drop a veil over it: sorrier misery was seldom enacted in the world. This one small fact, does it not throw the saddest light on much? The Queen is lamenting to Madam Campan: "What am I to do? When they, these Barnaves, get us advised to any step which the Noblesse do not like, then I am pouted at; nobody comes to my card table; the King's Couchee is solitary."

The King has accepted this Constitution, knowing beforehand that it will not serve: he studies it, and executes it in the hope mainly that it will be found inexecutable. King's Ships lie rotting in harbour, their officers gone; the Armies disorganised; robbers scour the highways, which wear down unrepaired; all Public Service lies slack and waste: the Executive makes no effort, or an effort only to throw the blame on the Constitution. Shamming death, 'faisant le mort!' What Constitution, use it in this manner, can march? 'Grow to disgust the Nation' it will truly, unless you first grow to disgust the Nation! It is Bertrand de Moleville's plan, and his Majesty's; the best they can form.

Or if, after all, this best-plan proved too slow; proved a failure? Provident of that too, the Queen, shrouded in deepest mystery, 'writes all day, in cipher, day after day, to Coblentz;' Engineer Goguelat, he of the Night of Spurs, whom the Lafayette Amnesty has delivered from Prison, rides and runs. Now and then, on fit occasion, a Royal familiar visit can be paid to that Salle de Manege, an affecting encouraging Royal Speech (sincere, doubt it not, for the moment) can be delivered there, and the Senators all cheer and almost weep; – at the same time Mallet du Pan has visibly ceased editing, and invisibly bears abroad a King's Autograph, soliciting help from the Foreign Potentates. Unhappy Louis, do this thing or else that other, – if thou couldst!

The thing which the King's Government did do was to stagger distractedly from contradiction to contradiction; and wedding Fire to Water, envelope itself in hissing, and ashy steam! Danton and needy corruptible Patriots are sopped with presents of cash: they accept the sop: they rise refreshed by it, and travel their own way. Nay, the King's Government did likewise hire Hand-clappers, or claqueurs, persons to applaud. Subterranean Rivarol has Fifteen Hundred men in King's pay, at the rate of some ten thousand pounds sterling, per month; what he calls 'a staff of genius:' Paragraph-writers, Placard-Journalists; 'two hundred and eighty Applauders, at three shillings a day:' one of the strangest Staffs ever commanded by man. The muster-rolls and account-books of which still exist. Bertrand-Moleville himself, in a way he thinks very dexterous, contrives to pack the Galleries of the Legislative; gets Sansculottes hired to go thither, and applaud at a signal given, they fancying it was Petion that bid them: a device which was not detected for almost a week. Dexterous enough; as if a man finding the Day fast decline should determine on altering the Clockhands: that is a thing possible for him.

THE STEEPLES AT MIDNIGHT, 1792.

For, in truth, the Insurrection is just about ripe. Thursday is the ninth of the month August: if Forfeiture be not pronounced by the Legislature that day, we must pronounce it ourselves.

Legislature? A poor waterlogged Legislature can pronounce nothing. On Wednesday the eighth, after endless oratory once again, they cannot even pronounce Accusation again Lafayette; but absolve him, – hear it, Patriotism! – by a majority of two to one. Patriotism hears it; Patriotism, hounded on by Prussian Terror, by Preternatural Suspicion, roars tumultuous round the Salle de Manege, all day; insults many leading Deputies, of the absolvent Right-side; nay chases them, collars them with loud menace: Deputy Vaublanc, and others of the like, are glad to take refuge in Guardhouses, and escape by the back window. And so, next day, there is infinite complaint; Letter after Letter from insulted Deputy; mere complaint, debate and self-cancelling jargon: the sun of Thursday sets like the others, and no Forfeiture pronounced. Wherefore in fine, To your tents, O Israel!

The Mother-Society ceases speaking; groups cease haranguing: Patriots, with closed lips now, 'take one another's arm;' walk off, in rows, two and two, at a brisk business-pace; and vanish afar in the obscure places of the East. Santerre is ready; or we will make him ready. Forty-seven of the Forty-eight Sections are ready; nay Filles-Saint-Thomas itself turns up the Jacobin side of it, turns down the Feuillant side of it, and is ready too. Let the unlimited Patriot look to his weapon, be it pike, be it firelock; and the Brest brethren, above all, the blackbrowed Marseillese prepare themselves for the extreme hour! Syndic Roederer knows, and laments or not as the issue may turn, that 'five thousand ball-cartridges, within these few days, have been distributed to Federes, at the Hotel-de-Ville.'

And ye likewise, gallant gentlemen, defenders of Royalty, crowd ye on your side to the Tuileries. Not to a Levee: no, to a Couchee: where much will be put to bed. Your Tickets of Entry are needful; needfuller your blunderbusses! – They come and crowd, like gallant men who also know how to die: old Maille the Camp-Marshal has come, his eyes gleaming once again, though dimmed by the rheum of almost fourscore years. Courage, Brothers! We have a thousand red Swiss; men stanch of heart, steadfast as the granite of their Alps. National Grenadiers are at least friends of Order; Commandant Mandat breathes loyal ardour, will "answer for it on his head." Mandat will, and his Staff; for the Staff, though there stands a doom and Decree to that effect, is happily never yet dissolved.

Commandant Mandat has corresponded with Mayor Petion; carries a written Order from him these three days, to repel force by force. A squadron on the Pont Neuf with cannon shall turn back these Marseillese coming across the River: a squadron at the Townhall shall cut Saint-Antoine in two, 'as it issues from the Arcade Saint-Jean;' drive one half back to the obscure East, drive the other half forward through 'the Wickets of the Louvre.' Squadrons not a few, and mounted squadrons; squadrons in the Palais Royal, in the Place Vendome: all these shall charge, at the right moment; sweep this street, and then sweep that. Some new Twentieth of June we shall have; only still more ineffectual? Or probably the Insurrection will not dare to rise at all? Mandat's Squadrons, Horse-Gendarmerie and blue Guards march, clattering, tramping; Mandat's Cannoneers rumble. Under cloud of night; to the sound of his generale, which begins drumming when men should go to bed. It is the 9th night of August, 1792.

On the other hand, the Forty-eight Sections correspond by swift messengers; are choosing each their 'three Delegates with full powers.' Syndic Roederer, Mayor Petion are sent for to the Tuileries: courageous Legislators, when the drum beats danger, should repair to their Salle. Demoiselle Theroigne has on her grenadier-bonnet, short-skirted riding-habit; two pistols garnish her small waist, and sabre hangs in baldric by her side.

Such a game is playing in this Paris Pandemonium, or City of All the Devils! – And yet the Night, as Mayor Petion walks here in the Tuileries Garden, 'is beautiful and calm;' Orion and the Pleiades glitter down quite serene. Petion has come forth, the 'heat' inside was so oppressive. Indeed, his Majesty's reception of him was of the roughest; as it well might be. And now there is no outgate; Mandat's blue Squadrons turn you back at every Grate; nay the Filles-Saint-Thomas Grenadiers give themselves liberties of tongue, How a virtuous Mayor 'shall pay for it, if there be mischief,' and the like; though others again are full of civility. Surely if any man in France is in straights this night, it is Mayor Petion: bound, under pain of death, one may say, to smile dexterously with the one side of his face, and weep with the other; – death if he do it not dexterously enough! Not till four in the morning does a National Assembly, hearing of his plight, summon him over 'to give account of Paris;' of which he knows nothing: whereby however he shall get home to bed, and only his gilt coach be left. Scarcely less delicate is Syndic Roederer's task; who must wait whether he will lament or not, till he see the issue. Janus Bifrons, or Mr. Facing-both-ways, as vernacular Bunyan has it! They walk there, in the meanwhile, these two Januses, with others of the like double conformation; and 'talk of indifferent matters.'

Roederer, from time to time, steps in; to listen, to speak; to send for the Department-Directory itself, he their

Procureur Syndic not seeing how to act. The Apartments are all crowded; some seven hundred gentlemen in black elbowing, bustling; red Swiss standing like rocks; ghost, or partial-ghost of a Ministry, with Roederer and advisers, hovering round their Majesties; old Marshall Maille kneeling at the King's feet, to say, He and these gallant gentlemen are come to die for him. List! through the placid midnight; clang of the distant stormbell! So, in very sooth; steeple after steeple takes up the wondrous tale. Black Courtiers listen at the windows, opened for air; discriminate the steeple-bells: this is the tocsin of Saint-Roch; that again, is it not Saint-Jacques, named de la Boucherie? Yes, Messieurs! Or even Saint-Germain l'Auxerrois, hear ye it not? The same metal that rang storm, two hundred and twenty years ago; but by a Majesty's order then; on Saint-Bartholomew's Eve (24th August, 1572.) – So go the steeple-bells; which Courtiers can discriminate. Nay, meseems, there is the Townhall itself; we know it by its sound! Yes, Friends, that is the Townhall; discoursing so, to the Night. Miraculously; by miraculous metal-tongue and man's arm: Marat himself, if you knew it, is pulling at the rope there! Marat is pulling; Robespierre lies deep, invisible for the next forty hours; and some men have heart, and some have as good as none, and not even frenzy will give them any.

What struggling confusion, as the issue slowly draws on; and the doubtful Hour, with pain and blind struggle, brings forth its Certainty, never to be abolished! – The Full-power Delegates, three from each Section, a Hundred and forty-four in all, got gathered at the Townhall, about midnight. Mandat's Squadron, stationed there, did not hinder their entering: are they not the 'Central Committee of the Sections' who sit here usually; though in greater number tonight? They are there: presided by Confusion, Irresolution, and the Clack of Tongues. Swift scouts fly; Rumour buzzes, of black Courtiers, red Swiss, of Mandat and his Squadrons that shall charge. Better put off the Insurrection? Yes, put it off. Ha, hark! Saint-Antoine booming out eloquent tocsin, of its own accord! – Friends, no: ye cannot put off the Insurrection; but must put it on, and live with it, or die with it.

Swift now, therefore: let these actual Old Municipals, on sight of the Full-powers, and mandate of the Sovereign elective People, lay down their functions; and this New Hundred and forty-four take them up! Will ye nill ye, worthy Old Municipals, ye must go. Nay is it not a happiness for many a Municipal that he can wash his hands of such a business; and sit there paralyzed, unaccountable, till the Hour do bring forth; or even go home to his night's rest? (Section Documents, Townhall Documents, Hist. Parl. ubi supra.) Two only of the Old, or at most three, we retain Mayor Petion, for the present walking in the Tuileries; Procureur Manuel; Procureur Substitute Danton, invisible Atlas of the whole. And so, with our Hundred and forty-four, among whom are a Tocsin-Huguenin, a Billaud, a Chaumette; and Editor-Talliens, and Fabre d'Eglantines, Sergents, Panises; and in brief, either emergent, or else emerged and full-blown, the entire Flower of unlimited Patriotism: have we not, as by magic, made a New Municipality; ready to act in the unlimited manner; and declare itself roundly, 'in a State of Insurrection!' – First of all, then, be Commandant Mandat sent for, with that Mayor's-Order of his; also let the New Municipals visit those Squadrons that were to charge; and let the stormbell ring its loudest; – and, on the whole,

Forward, ye Hundred and forty-four; retreat is now none for you!

Reader, fancy not, in thy languid way, that Insurrection is easy. Insurrection is difficult: each individual uncertain even of his next neighbour; totally uncertain of his distant neighbours, what strength is with him, what strength is against him; certain only that, in case of failure, his individual portion is the gallows! Eight hundred thousand heads, and in each of them a separate estimate of these uncertainties, a separate theorem of action conformable to that: out of so many uncertainties, does the certainty, and inevitable net-result never to be abolished, go on, at all moments, bodying itself forth; – leading thee also towards civic-crowns or an ignominious noose.

Could the Reader take an Asmodeus's Flight, and waving open all roofs and privacies, look down from the Tower of Notre Dame, what a Paris were it! Of treble-voice whimperings or vehemence, of bass-voice growlings, dubitations; Courage screwing itself to desperate defiance; Cowardice trembling silent within barred doors; – and all round, Dulness calmly snoring; for much Dulness, flung on its mattresses, always sleeps. O, between the clangour of these high-storming tocsins and that snore of Dulness, what a gamut: of trepidation, excitation, desperation; and above it mere Doubt, Danger, Atropos and Nox!

Fighters of this section draw out; hear that the next Section does not; and thereupon draw in. Saint-Antoine, on this side the River, is uncertain of Saint-Marceau on that. Steady only is the snore of Dulness, are the Six Hundred Marseillese that know how to die! Mandat, twice summoned to the Townhall, has not come. Scouts fly incessant, in distracted haste; and the many-whispering voices of Rumour. Theroigne and unofficial Patriots flit, dim-visible, exploratory, far and wide; like Night-birds on the wing. Of Nationals some Three thousand have followed Mandat and his generale; the rest follow each his own theorem of the uncertainties: theorem, that one should march rather with Saint-Antoine; innumerable theorems, that in such a case the wholesomest were sleep. And so the drums beat, in made fits, and the stormbells peal. Saint-Antoine itself does but draw out and draw in; Commandant Santerre, over there, cannot believe that the Marseillese and Saint Marceau will march. Thou laggard sonorous Beer-vat, with the loud voice and timber head, is it time now to palter? Alsatian Westermann clutches him by the throat with drawn sabre: whereupon the Timber-headed believes. In this manner wanes the slow night; amid fret, uncertainty and tocsin; all men's humour rising to the hysterical pitch; and nothing done.

However, Mandat, on the third summons does come; – come, unguarded; astonished to find the Municipality new. They question him straitly on that Mayor's-Order to resist force by force; on that strategic scheme of cutting Saint-Antoine in two halves: he answers what he can: they think it were right to send this strategic National Commandant to the Abbaye Prison, and let a Court of Law decide on him. Alas, a Court of Law, not Book-Law but primeval Club-Law, crowds and jostles out of doors; all fretted to the hysterical pitch; cruel as Fear, blind as the Night: such Court of Law, and no other, clutches poor Mandat from his constables; beats him down, massacres him, on the steps of the Townhall. Look to it, ye new Municipals; ye People, in a state of Insurrection! Blood is shed, blood must be answered for; – alas, in such hysterical humour, more blood will flow: for it is as with the Tiger in that; he has only to begin.

Seventeen Individuals have been seized in the Champs Elysees, by exploratory Patriotism; they flitting dim-visible, by it flitting dim-visible. Ye have pistols, rapiers, ye Seventeen? One of those accursed 'false Patrols;' that go marauding, with Anti-National intent; seeking what they can spy, what they can spill! The Seventeen are carried to the nearest Guard-house; eleven of them escape by back passages. "How is this?" Demoiselle Theroigne appears at the front entrance, with sabre, pistols, and a train; denounces treasonous connivance; demands, seizes, the remaining six, that the justice of the People be not trifled with. Of which six two more escape in the whirl and debate of the Club-Law Court; the last unhappy Four are massacred, as Mandat was: Two Ex-Bodyguards; one dissipated Abbe; one Royalist Pamphleteer, Sulleau, known to us by name, Able Editor, and wit of all work. Poor Sulleau: his Acts of the Apostles, and brisk Placard-Journals (for he was an able man) come to Finis, in this manner; and questionable jesting issues suddenly in horrid earnest! Such doings usher in the dawn of the Tenth of August, 1792.

Or think what a night the poor National Assembly has had: sitting there, 'in great paucity,' attempting to debate; – quivering and shivering; pointing towards all the thirty-two azimuths at once, as the magnet-needle does when thunderstorm is in the air! If the Insurrection come? If it come, and fail? Alas, in that case, may not black Courtiers, with blunderbusses, red Swiss with bayonets rush over, flushed with victory, and ask us: Thou undefinable, waterlogged, self-distractive, self-destructive Legislative, what dost thou here unsunk? – Or figure the poor National Guards, bivouacking 'in temporary tents' there; or standing ranked, shifting from leg to leg, all through the weary night; New tricolor Municipals ordering one thing, old Mandat Captains ordering another! Procureur Manuel has ordered the cannons to be withdrawn from the Pont Neuf; none ventured to disobey him. It seemed certain, then, the old Staff so long doomed has finally been dissolved, in these hours; and Mandat is not our Commandant now, but Santerre? Yes, friends: Santerre henceforth, – surely Mandat no more! The Squadrons that were to charge see nothing certain, except that they are cold, hungry, worn down with watching; that it were sad to slay French brothers; sadder to be slain by them. Without the Tuileries Circuit, and within it, sour uncertain humour sways these men: only the red Swiss stand steadfast. Them their officers refresh now with a slight wetting of brandy; wherein the Nationals, too far gone for brandy, refuse to participate.

King Louis meanwhile had laid him down for a little sleep: his wig when he reappeared had lost the powder on one side. Old Marshal Maille and the gentlemen in black rise always in spirits, as the Insurrection does not rise: there goes a witty saying now, "Le tocsin ne rend pas." The tocsin, like a dry milk-cow, does not yield. For the rest, could one not proclaim Martial Law? Not easily; for now, it seems, Mayor Petion is gone. On the other hand, our Interim Commandant, poor Mandat being off, 'to the Hotel-de-Ville,' complains that so many Courtiers in black encumber the service, are an eyesorrow to the National Guards. To which her Majesty answers with emphasis, That they will obey all, will suffer all, that they are sure men these.

And so the yellow lamplight dies out in the gray of morning, in the King's Palace, over such a scene. Scene of jostling, elbowing, of confusion, and indeed conclusion, for the thing is about to end. Roederer and spectral Ministers jostle in the press; consult, in side cabinets, with one or with both Majesties. Sister Elizabeth takes the Queen to the window: "Sister, see what a beautiful sunrise," right over the Jacobins church and that quarter! How happy if the tocsin did not yield! But Mandat returns not; Petion is gone: much hangs wavering in the invisible Balance. About five o'clock, there rises from the Garden a kind of sound; as of a shout to which had become a howl, and instead of Vive le Roi were ending in Vive la Nation. "Mon Dieu!" ejaculates a spectral Minister, "what is he doing down there?" For it is his Majesty, gone down with old Marshal Maille to review the troops; and the nearest companies of them answer so. Her Majesty bursts into a stream of tears. Yet on stepping from the cabinet her eyes are dry and calm, her look is even cheerful. 'The Austrian lip, and the aquiline nose, fuller than usual, gave to her countenance,' says Peltier, (in Toulongeon, ii. 241.) 'something of Majesty, which they that did not see her in these moments cannot well have an idea of.' O thou Theresa's Daughter!

King Louis enters, much blown with the fatigue; but for the rest with his old air of indifference. Of all hopes now surely the joyfullest were, that the tocsin did not yield.

THE SWISS.

Unhappy Friends, the tocsin does yield, has yielded! Lo ye, how with the first sun-rays its Ocean-tide, of pikes and fusils, flows glittering from the far East; – immeasurable; born of the Night! They march there, the grim host; Saint-Antoine on this side of the River; Saint-Marceau on that, the blackbrowed Marseillese in the van. With hum, and grim murmur, far-heard; like the Ocean-tide, as we say: drawn up, as if by Luna and Influences, from the great Deep of Waters, they roll gleaming on; no King, Canute or Louis, can bid them roll back. Wide-eddying side-currents, of onlookers, roll hither and thither, unarmed, not voiceless; they, the steel host, roll on. New-Commandant Santerre, indeed, has taken seat at the Townhall; rests there, in his half-way-house. Alsatian Westermann, with flashing sabre, does not rest; nor the Sections, nor the Marseillese, nor Demoiselle Theroigne; but roll continually on.

And now, where are Mandat's Squadrons that were to charge? Not a Squadron of them stirs: or they stir in the wrong direction, out of the way; their officers glad that they will even do that. It is to this hour uncertain whether the Squadron on the Pont Neuf made the shadow of resistance, or did not make the shadow: enough, the blackbrowed Marseillese, and Saint-Marceau following them, do cross without let; do cross, in sure hope now of Saint-Antoine and the rest; do billow on, towards the Tuileries, where their errand is. The Tuileries, at sound of them, rustles responsive: the red Swiss look to their priming; Courtiers in black draw their blunderbusses, rapiers, poniards, some have even fire-shovels; every man his weapon of war.

Judge if, in these circumstances, Syndic Roederer felt easy! Will the kind Heavens open no middle-course of refuge for a poor Syndic who halts between two? If indeed his Majesty would consent to go over to the Assembly! His Majesty, above all her Majesty, cannot agree to that. Did her Majesty answer the proposal with a "Fi donc;" did she say even, she would be nailed to the walls sooner? Apparently not. It is written also that she offered the King a pistol; saying, Now or else never was the time to shew himself. Close eye-witnesses did not see it, nor do we. That saw only that she was queenlike, quiet; that she argued not, upbraided not, with the Inexorable; but, like Caesar in the Capitol, wrapped her mantle, as it beseems Queens and Sons of Adam to do. But thou, O Louis! of what stuff art thou at all? Is there no stroke in thee, then, for Life and Crown? The silliest hunted deer dies not so. Art thou the languidest of all mortals; or the mildest-minded? Thou art the worst-starred.

The tide advances; Syndic Roederer's and all men's straits grow straiter and straiter. Fremescent clangor comes from the armed Nationals in the Court; far and wide is the infinite hubbub of tongues. What counsel? And the tide is now nigh! Messengers, forerunners speak hastily through the outer Grates; hold parley sitting astride the walls. Syndic Roederer goes out and comes in. Cannoneers ask him: Are we to fire against the people? King's Ministers ask him: Shall the King's House be forced? Syndic Roederer has a hard game to play. He speaks to the Cannoneers with eloquence, with fervour; such fervour as a man can, who has to blow hot and cold in one breath. Hot and cold, O Roederer? We, for our part, cannot live and die! The Cannoneers, by way of answer, fling down their linstocks. – Think of this answer, O King Louis, and King's Ministers: and take a poor Syndic's safe middle-course, towards the Salle de Manege. King Louis sits, his hands leant on knees, body bent forward; gazes for a space fixedly on Syndic Roederer; then answers, looking over his shoulder to the Queen: Marchons! They march; King Louis, Queen, Sister Elizabeth, the two royal children and governess: these, with Syndic Roederer, and Officials of the Department; amid a double rank of National Guards. The men with blunderbusses, the steady red Swiss gaze mournfully, reproachfully; but hear only these words from Syndic Roederer: "The King is going to the Assembly; make way." It has struck eight, on all clocks, some minutes ago: the King has left the Tuileries – for ever.

O ye staunch Swiss, ye gallant gentlemen in black, for what a cause are ye to spend and be spent! Look out from the western windows, ye may see King Louis placidly hold on his way; the poor little Prince Royal 'sportfully kicking the fallen leaves.' Fremescent multitude on the Terrace of the Feuillants whirls parallel to him; one man in it, very noisy, with a long pole: will they not obstruct the outer Staircase, and back-entrance of the Salle, when it comes to that? King's Guards can go no further than the bottom step there. Lo, Deputation of Legislators come out; he of the long pole is stilled by oratory; Assembly's Guards join themselves to King's Guards, and all may mount in this case of necessity; the outer Staircase is free, or passable. See, Royalty ascends; a blue Grenadier lifts the poor little Prince Royal from the press; Royalty has entered in. Royalty has vanished for ever from your eyes. – And ye? Left standing there, amid the yawning abysses, and earthquake of Insurrection; without course; without command: if ye perish it must be as more than martyrs, as martyrs who are now without a cause! The black Courtiers disappear mostly; through such issues as they can. The poor Swiss know not how to act: one duty only is clear to them, that of standing by their post; and they will perform that.

But the glittering steel tide has arrived; it beats now against the Chateau barriers, and eastern Courts; irresistible, loud-surging far and wide; – breaks in, fills the Court of the Carrousel, blackbrowed Marseillese in the van. King Louis gone, say you; over to the Assembly! Well and good: but till the Assembly pronounce Forfeiture of him, what boots it? Our post is in that Chateau or stronghold of his; there till then must we continue. Think, ye stanch Swiss, whether it were good that grim murder began, and brothers blasted one another in pieces for a stone edifice? – Poor Swiss! they know not how to act: from the southern windows, some fling cartridges, in sign of brotherhood; on the eastern outer staircase, and within through long stairs and corridors, they stand firm-ranked, peaceable and yet refusing to stir. Westermann speaks to them in Alsatian German; Marseillese plead, in hot Provencal speech and pantomime; stunning hubbub pleads and threatens, infinite, around. The Swiss stand fast, peaceable and yet immovable; red granite pier in that waste-flashing sea of steel.

Who can help the inevitable issue; Marseillese and all France, on this side; granite Swiss on that? The pantomime grows hotter and hotter; Marseillese sabres flourishing by way of action; the Swiss brow also clouding itself, the Swiss thumb bringing its firelock to the cock. And hark! high-thundering above all the din, three Marseillese cannon from the Carrousel, pointed by a gunner of bad aim, come rattling over the roofs! Ye Swiss, therefore: Fire! The Swiss fire; by volley, by platoon, in rolling-fire: Marseillese men not a few, and 'a tall man that was louder than any,' lie silent, smashed, upon the pavement; – not a few Marseillese, after the long dusty march, have made halt here. The Carrousel is void; the black tide recoiling; 'fugitives rushing as far as Saint-Antoine before they stop.' The Cannoneers without linstock have squatted invisible, and left their cannon; which the Swiss seize.

Think what a volley: reverberating doomful to the four corners of Paris, and through all hearts; like the clang of Bellona's thongs! The blackbrowed Marseillese, rallying on the instant, have become black Demons that know how to die. Nor is Brest behind-hand; nor Alsatian Westermann; Demoiselle Theroigne is Sybil Theroigne: Vengeance Victoire, ou la mort! From all Patriot artillery, great and small; from Feuillants Terrace, and all terraces and places of the widespread Insurrectionary sea, there roars responsive a red whirlwind. Blue Nationals, ranked in the Garden, cannot help their muskets going off, against Foreign murderers. For there is a sympathy in muskets, in heaped masses of men: nay, are not Mankind, in whole, like tuned strings, and a cunning infinite concordance and unity; you smite one string, and all strings will begin sounding, – in soft sphere-melody, in deafening screech of madness! Mounted Gendarmerie gallop distracted; are fired on merely as a thing running; galloping over the Pont Royal, or one knows not whither. The brain of Paris, brain-fevered in the centre of it here, has gone mad; what you call, taken fire.

Behold, the fire slackens not; nor does the Swiss rolling-fire slacken from within. Nay they clutched cannon, as we saw: and now, from the other side, they clutch three pieces more; alas, cannon without linstock; nor will the steel-and-flint answer, though they try it. Had it chanced to answer! Patriot onlookers have their misgivings; one strangest Patriot onlooker thinks that the Swiss, had they a commander, would beat. He is a man not unqualified to judge; the name of him is Napoleon Buonaparte. And onlookers, and women, stand gazing, and the witty Dr. Moore of Glasgow among them, on the other side of the River: cannon rush rumbling past them; pause on the Pont Royal; belch out their iron entrails there, against the Tuileries; and at every new belch, the women and onlookers shout and clap hands. City of all the Devils! In remote streets, men are drinking breakfast-coffee; following their affairs; with a start now and then, as some dull echo reverberates a note louder. And here? Marseillese fall wounded; but Barbaroux has surgeons; Barbaroux is close by, managing, though underhand, and under cover. Marseillese fall death-struck; bequeath their firelock, specify in which pocket are the cartridges; and die, murmuring, "Revenge me, Revenge thy country!" Brest Federe Officers, galloping in red coats, are shot as Swiss. Lo you, the Carrousel has burst into flame! – Paris Pandemonium! Nay the poor City, as we said, is in fever-fit and convulsion; such crisis has lasted for the space of some half hour.

But what is this that, with Legislative Insignia, ventures through the hubbub and death-hail, from the back-entrance of the Manege? Towards the Tuileries and Swiss: written Order from his Majesty to cease firing! O ye hapless Swiss, why was there no order not to begin it? Gladly would the Swiss cease firing: but who will bid mad Insurrection cease firing? To Insurrection you cannot speak; neither can it, hydra-headed, hear. The dead and dying, by the hundred, lie all around; are borne bleeding through the streets, towards help; the sight of them, like a torch of the Furies, kindling Madness. Patriot Paris roars; as the bear bereaved of her whelps. On, ye Patriots: vengeance! victory or death! There are men seen, who rush on, armed only with walking-sticks. Terror and Fury rule the hour.

The Swiss, pressed on from without, paralyzed from within, have ceased to shoot; but not to be shot. What shall they do? Desperate is the moment. Shelter or instant death: yet How? Where? One party flies out by the Rue de l'Echelle; is destroyed utterly, 'en entier.' A second, by the other side, throws itself into the Garden; 'hurrying across a keen fusillade:' rushes suppliant into the National Assembly; finds pity and refuge in the back benches there. The third, and largest, darts out in column, three hundred strong, towards the Champs Elysees: Ah, could we but reach Courbevoye, where other Swiss are! Wo! see, in such fusillade the column 'soon breaks itself by diversity of opinion,' into distracted segments, this way and that; – to escape in holes, to die fighting from street to street. The firing and murdering will not cease; not yet for long. The red Porters of Hotels are shot at, be they Suisse by nature, or Suisse only in name. The very Firemen, who pump and labour on that smoking Carrousel, are shot at; why should the Carrousel not burn? Some Swiss take refuge in private houses; find that mercy too does still dwell in the heart of man. The brave Marseillese are merciful, late so wroth; and labour to save. Journalist Gorsas pleads hard with enfuriated groups. Clemence, the Wine-merchant, stumbles forward to the Bar of the Assembly, a rescued Swiss in his hand; tells passionately how he rescued him with pain and peril, how he will henceforth support him, being childless himself; and falls a swoon round the poor Swiss's neck: amid plaudits. But the most are butchered, and even mangled. Fifty (some say Fourscore) were marched as prisoners, by National Guards, to the Hotel-de-Ville: the ferocious people bursts through on them, in the Place de Greve; massacres them to the last man. 'O Peuple, envy of the universe!' Peuple, in mad Gaelic effervescence!

Surely few things in the history of carnage are painfuller. What ineffaceable red streak, flickering so sad in the memory, is that, of this poor column of red Swiss 'breaking itself in the confusion of opinions;' dispersing, into blackness and death! Honour to you, brave men; honourable pity, through long times! Not martyrs were ye; and yet almost more. He was no King of yours, this Louis; and he forsook you like a King of shreds and patches; ye were but sold to him for some poor sixpence a-day; yet would ye work for your wages, keep your plighted word. The work now was to die; and ye did it. Honour to you, O Kinsmen; and may the old Deutsch Biederheit and Tapferkeit, and Valour which is Worth and Truth be they Swiss, be they Saxon, fail in no age! Not bastards; true-born were these men; sons of the men of Sempach, of Murten, who knelt, but not to thee, O Burgundy! – Let the traveller, as he passes through Lucerne, turn aside to look a little at their monumental Lion; not for Thorwaldsen's sake alone. Hewn out of living rock, the Figure rests there, by the still Lake-waters, in lullaby of distant-tinkling rance-des-vaches, the granite Mountains dumbly keeping watch all round; and, though inanimate, speaks.

CONSTITUTION BURST IN PIECES.

Thus is the Tenth of August won and lost. Patriotism reckons its slain by thousand on thousand, so deadly was the Swiss fire from these windows; but will finally reduce them to some Twelve hundred. No child's play was it; – nor is it! Till two in the afternoon the massacring, the breaking and the burning has not ended; nor the loose Bedlam shut itself again.

How deluges of frantic Sansculottism roared through all passages of this Tuileries, ruthless in vengeance, how the Valets were butchered, hewn down; and Dame Campan saw the Marseilles sabre flash over her head, but the Blackbrowed said, "Va-t-en, Get thee gone," and flung her from him unstruck: how in the cellars wine-bottles were broken, wine-butts were staved in and drunk; and, upwards to the very garrets, all windows tumbled out their precious royal furnitures; and, with gold mirrors, velvet curtains, down of ript feather-beds, and dead bodies of men, the Tuileries was like no Garden of the Earth: – all this let him who has a taste for it see amply in Mercier, in acrid Montgaillard, or Beaulieu of the Deux Amis. A hundred and eighty bodies of Swiss lie piled there; naked, unremoved till the second day. Patriotism has torn their red coats into snips; and marches with them at the Pike's point: the ghastly bare corpses lie there, under the sun and under the stars; the curious of both sexes crowding to look. Which let not us do. Above a hundred carts heaped with Dead fare towards the Cemetery of Sainte-Madeleine; bewailed, bewept; for all had kindred, all had mothers, if not here, then there. It is one of those Carnage-fields, such as you read of by the name 'Glorious Victory,' brought home in this case to one's own door.

But the blackbrowed Marseillese have struck down the Tyrant of the Chateau. He is struck down; low, and hardly to rise. What a moment for an august Legislative was that when the Hereditary Representative entered, under such circumstances; and the Grenadier, carrying the little Prince Royal out of the Press, set him down on the Assembly-table! A moment, – which one had to smooth off with oratory; waiting what the next would bring! Louis said few words: "He was come hither to prevent a great crime; he believed himself safer nowhere than here." President Vergniaud answered briefly, in vague oratory as we say, about "defence of Constituted Authorities," about dying at our post. And so King Louis sat him down; first here, then there; for a difficulty arose, the Constitution not permitting us to debate while the King is present: finally he settles himself with his Family in the 'Loge of the Logographe' in the Reporter's-Box of a Journalist: which is beyond the enchanted Constitutional Circuit, separated from it by a rail. To such Lodge of the Logographe, measuring some ten feet square, with a small closet at the entrance of it behind, is the King of broad France now limited: here can he and his sit pent, under the eyes of the world, or retire into their closet at intervals; for the space of sixteen hours. Such quiet peculiar moment has the Legislative lived to see.

But also what a moment was that other, few minutes later, when the three Marseillese cannon went off, and the Swiss rolling-fire and universal thunder, like the Crack of Doom, began to rattle! Honourable Members start to their feet; stray bullets singing epicedium even here, shivering in with window-glass and jingle. "No, this is our post; let us die here!" They sit therefore, like stone Legislators. But may not the Lodge of the Logographe be forced from behind? Tear down the railing that divides it from the enchanted Constitutional Circuit! Ushers tear and tug; his Majesty himself aiding from within: the railing gives way; Majesty and Legislative are united in place, unknown Destiny hovering over both.

Rattle, and again rattle, went the thunder; one breathless wide-eyed messenger rushing in after another: King's orders to the Swiss went out. It was a fearful thunder; but, as we know, it ended. Breathless messengers, fugitive Swiss, denunciatory Patriots, trepidation; finally tripudiation! – Before four o'clock much has come and gone.

The New Municipals have come and gone; with Three Flags, Liberte, Egalite, Patrie, and the clang of vivats. Vergniaud, he who as President few hours ago talked of Dying for Constituted Authorities, has moved, as Committee-Reporter, that the Hereditary Representative be suspended; that a NATIONAL CONVENTION do forthwith assemble to say what further! An able Report: which the President must have had ready in his pocket? A President, in such cases, must have much ready, and yet not ready; and Janus-like look before and after.

King Louis listens to all; retires about midnight 'to three little rooms on the upper floor;' till the Luxembourg be prepared for him, and 'the safeguard of the Nation.' Safer if Brunswick were once here! Or, alas, not so safe? Ye hapless discrowned heads! Crowds came, next morning, to catch a glimpse of them, in their three upper rooms. Montgaillard says the august Captives wore an air of cheerfulness, even of gaiety; that the Queen and Princess Lamballe, who had joined her over night, looked out of the open window, 'shook powder from their hair on the people below, and laughed.' He is an acrid distorted man.

For the rest, one may guess that the Legislative, above all that the New Municipality continues busy. Messengers,

Municipal or Legislative, and swift despatches rush off to all corners of France; full of triumph, blended with indignant wail, for Twelve hundred have fallen. France sends up its blended shout responsive; the Tenth of August shall be as the Fourteenth of July, only bloodier and greater. The Court has conspired? Poor Court: the Court has been vanquished; and will have both the scath to bear and the scorn. How the Statues of Kings do now all fall! Bronze Henri himself, though he wore a cockade once, jingles down from the Pont Neuf, where Patrie floats in Danger. Much more does Louis Fourteenth, from the Place Vendome, jingle down, and even breaks in falling. The curious can remark, written on his horse's shoe: '12 Aout 1692;' a Century and a Day.

The Tenth of August was Friday. The week is not done, when our old Patriot Ministry is recalled, what of it can be got: strict Roland, Genevese Claviere; add heavy Monge the Mathematician, once a stone-hewer; and, for Minister of Justice, – Danton 'led hither,' as himself says, in one of his gigantic figures, 'through the breach of Patriot cannon!' These, under Legislative Committees, must rule the wreck as they can: confusedly enough; with an old Legislative waterlogged, with a New Municipality so brisk. But National Convention will get itself together; and then! Without delay, however, let a New Jury-Court and Criminal Tribunal be set up in Paris, to try the crimes and conspiracies of the Tenth. High Court of Orleans is distant, slow: the blood of the Twelve hundred Patriots, whatever become of other blood, shall be inquired after. Tremble, ye Criminals and Conspirators; the Minister of Justice is Danton! Robespierre too, after the victory, sits in the New Municipality; insurrectionary 'improvised Municipality,' which calls itself Council General of the Commune.

For three days now, Louis and his Family have heard the Legislative Debates in the Lodge of the Logographe; and retired nightly to their small upper rooms. The Luxembourg and safeguard of the Nation could not be got ready: nay, it seems the Luxembourg has too many cellars and issues; no Municipality can undertake to watch it. The compact Prison of the Temple, not so elegant indeed, were much safer. To the Temple, therefore! On Monday, 13th day of August 1792, in Mayor Petion's carriage, Louis and his sad suspended Household, fare thither; all Paris out to look at them. As they pass through the Place Vendome Louis Fourteenth's Statue lies broken on the ground. Petion is afraid the Queen's looks may be thought scornful, and produce provocation; she casts down her eyes, and does not look at all. The 'press is prodigious,' but quiet: here and there, it shouts Vive la Nation; but for most part gazes in silence. French Royalty vanishes within the gates of the Temple: these old peaked Towers, like peaked Extinguisher or Bonsoir, do cover it up; – from which same Towers, poor Jacques Molay and his Templars were burnt out, by French Royalty, five centuries since. Such are the turns of Fate below. Foreign Ambassadors, English Lord Gower have all demanded passports; are driving indignantly towards their respective homes.

So, then, the Constitution is over? For ever and a day! Gone is that wonder of the Universe; First biennial Parliament, waterlogged, waits only till the Convention come; and will then sink to endless depths.

PART III – THE GUILLOTINE

THE IMPROVISED COMMUNE.

Ye have roused her, then, ye Emigrants and Despots of the world; France is roused; long have ye been lecturing and tutoring this poor Nation, like cruel uncalled-for pedagogues, shaking over her your ferulas of fire and steel: it is long that ye have pricked and fillipped and affrighted her, there as she sat helpless in her dead cerements of a Constitution, you gathering in on her from all lands, with your armaments and plots, your invadings and truculent bullyings; – and lo now, ye have pricked her to the quick, and she is up, and her blood is up. The dead cerements are rent into cobwebs, and she fronts you in that terrible strength of Nature, which no man has measured, which goes down to Madness and Tophet: see now how ye will deal with her!

This month of September, 1792, which has become one of the memorable months of History, presents itself under two most diverse aspects; all of black on the one side, all of bright on the other. Whatsoever is cruel in the panic frenzy of Twenty-five million men, whatsoever is great in the simultaneous death-defiance of Twenty-five million men, stand here in abrupt contrast, near by one another. As indeed is usual when a man, how much more when a Nation of men, is hurled suddenly beyond the limits. For Nature, as green as she looks, rests everywhere on dread foundations, were we farther down; and Pan, to whose music the Nymphs

107

dance, has a cry in him that can drive all men distracted.

Very frightful it is when a Nation, rending asunder its Constitutions and Regulations which were grown dead cerements for it, becomes transcendental; and must now seek its wild way through the New, Chaotic, – where Force is not yet distinguished into Bidden and Forbidden, but Crime and Virtue welter unseparated, – in that domain of what is called the Passions; of what we call the Miracles and the Portents! It is thus that, for some three years to come, we are to contemplate France, in this final Third Volume of our History. Sansculottism reigning in all its grandeur and in all its hideousness: the Gospel (God's Message) of Man's Rights, Man's mights or strengths, once more preached irrefragably abroad; along with this, and still louder for the time, and fearfullest Devil's-Message of Man's weaknesses and sins; – and all on such a scale, and under such aspect: cloudy 'death-birth of a world;' huge smoke-cloud, streaked with rays as of heaven on one side; girt on the other as with hell-fire! History tells us many things: but for the last thousand years and more, what thing has she told us of a sort like this? Which therefore let us two, O Reader, dwell on willingly, for a little; and from its endless significance endeavour to extract what may, in present circumstances, be adapted for us.

It is unfortunate, though very natural, that the history of this Period has so generally been written in hysterics. Exaggeration abounds, execration, wailing; and, on the whole, darkness. But thus too, when foul old Rome had to be swept from the Earth, and those Northmen, and other horrid sons of Nature, came in, 'swallowing formulas' as the French now do, foul old Rome screamed execratively her loudest; so that, the true shape of many things is lost for us.

Attila's Huns had arms of such length that they could lift a stone without stooping. Into the body of the poor Tatars execrative Roman History intercalated an alphabetic letter; and so they continue Ta-r-tars, of fell Tartarean nature, to this day. Here, in like manner, search as we will in these multiform innumerable French Records, darkness too frequently covers, or sheer distraction bewilders. One finds it difficult to imagine that the Sun shone in this September month, as he does in others. Nevertheless it is an indisputable fact that the Sun did shine; and there was weather and work, – nay, as to that, very bad weather for harvest work! An unlucky Editor may do his utmost; and after all, require allowances.

Governing Persons, were they never so insignificant intrinsically, have for most part plenty of Memoir-writers; and the curious, in after-times, can learn minutely their goings out and comings in: which, as men always love to know their fellow-men in singular situations, is a comfort, of its kind. Not so, with these Governing Persons, now in the Townhall! And yet what most original fellow-man, of the Governing sort, high-chancellor, king, kaiser, secretary of the home or the foreign department, ever shewed such a phasis as Clerk Tallien, Procureur Manuel, future Procureur Chaumette, here in this Sand-waltz of the Twenty-five millions, now do? O brother mortals, – thou Advocate Panis, friend of Danton, kinsman of Santerre; Engraver Sergent, since called Agate Sergent; thou Huguenin, with the tocsin in thy heart! But, as Horace says, they wanted the sacred memoir-writer (sacro vate); and we know them not. Men bragged of August and its doings, publishing them in high places; but of this September none now or afterwards would brag. The September world remains dark, fuliginous, as Lapland witch-midnight; – from which, indeed, very strange shapes will evolve themselves.

Understand this, however: that incorruptible Robespierre is not wanting, now when the brunt of battle is past; in a stealthy way the seagreen man sits there, his feline eyes excellent in the twilight. Also understand this other, a single fact worth many: that Marat is not only there, but has a seat of honour assigned him, a tribune particuliere. How changed for Marat; lifted from his dark cellar into this luminous 'peculiar tribune!' All dogs have their day; even rabid dogs. Sorrowful, incurable Philoctetes Marat; without whom Troy cannot be taken! Hither, as a main element of the Governing Power, has Marat been raised. Royalist types, for we have 'suppressed' innumerable Durosoys, Royous, and even clapt them in prison, – Royalist types replace the worn types often snatched from a People's-Friend in old ill days. In our 'peculiar tribune' we write and redact: Placards, of due monitory terror; Amis-du-Peuple (now under the name of Journal de la Republique); and sit obeyed of men. 'Marat,' says one, 'is the conscience of the Hotel-de-Ville.' Keeper, as some call it, of the Sovereign's Conscience; – which surely, in such hands, will not lie hid in a napkin!

DUMOURIEZ.

Such are the last days of August, 1792; days gloomy, disastrous, and of evil omen. What will become of this poor France? Dumouriez rode from the Camp of Maulde, eastward to Sedan, on Tuesday last, the 28th of the month; reviewed that so-called Army left forlorn there by Lafayette:

the forlorn soldiers gloomed on him; were heard growling on him, "This is one of them, ce b – e la, that made War be declared." Unpromising Army! Recruits flow in, filtering through Depot after Depot; but recruits merely: in want of all; happy if they have so much as arms. And Longwi has fallen basely; and Brunswick, and the Prussian King, with his sixty thousand, will beleaguer Verdun; and Clairfait and Austrians press deeper in, over the Northern marches: 'a hundred and fifty thousand' as fear counts, 'eighty thousand' as the returns shew, do hem us in; Cimmerian Europe behind them. There is Castries-and-Broglie chivalry; Royalist foot 'in red facing and nankeen trousers;' breathing death and the gallows.

And lo, finally! at Verdun on Sunday the 2d of September 1792, Brunswick is here. With his King and sixty thousand, glittering over the heights, from beyond the winding Meuse River, he looks down on us, on our 'high citadel' and all our confectionery-ovens (for we are celebrated for confectionery) has sent courteous summons, in order to spare the effusion of blood! – Resist him to the death? Every day of retardation precious? How, O General Beaurepaire (asks the amazed Municipality) shall we resist him? We, the Verdun Municipals, see no resistance possible. Has he not sixty thousand, and artillery without end? Retardation, Patriotism is good; but so likewise is peaceable baking of pastry, and sleeping in whole skin. – Hapless Beaurepaire stretches out his hands, and pleads passionately, in the name of country, honour, of Heaven and of Earth: to no purpose. The Municipals have, by law, the power of ordering it; – with an Army officered by Royalism or Crypto-Royalism, such a Law seemed needful: and they order it, as pacific

Pastrycooks, not as heroic Patriots would, – To surrender! Beaurepaire strides home, with long steps: his valet, entering the room, sees him 'writing eagerly,' and withdraws. His valet hears then, in a few minutes, the report of a pistol: Beaurepaire is lying dead; his eager writing had been a brief suicidal farewell. In this manner died Beaurepaire, wept of France; buried in the Pantheon, with honourable pension to his Widow, and for Epitaph these words, He chose Death rather than yield to Despots. The Prussians, descending from the heights, are peaceable masters of Verdun.

And so Brunswick advances, from stage to stage: who shall now stay him, – covering forty miles of country? Foragers fly far; the villages of the North-East are harried; your Hessian forager has only 'three sous a day:' the very Emigrants, it is said, will take silver-plate, – by way of revenge. Clermont, Sainte-Menehould, Varennes especially, ye Towns of the Night of Spurs; tremble ye! Procureur Sausse and the Magistracy of Varennes have fled; brave Boniface Le Blanc of the Bras d'Or is to the woods: Mrs. Le Blanc, a young woman fair to look upon, with her young infant, has to live in greenwood, like a beautiful Bessy Bell of Song, her bower thatched with rushes; – catching premature rheumatism. Clermont may ring the tocsin now, and illuminate itself! Clermont lies at the foot of its Cow (or Vache, so they name that Mountain), a prey to the Hessian spoiler: its fair women, fairer than most, are robbed: not of life, or what is dearer, yet of all that is cheaper and portable; for Necessity, on three half-pence a-day, has no law. At Saint-Menehould, the enemy has been expected more than once, – our Nationals all turning out in arms; but was not yet seen. Post-master Drouet, he is not in the woods, but minding his Election;

and will sit in the Convention, notable King-taker, and bold Old-Dragoon as he is.

Thus on the North-East all roams and runs; and on a set day, the date of which is irrecoverable by History, Brunswick 'has engaged to dine in Paris,' – the Powers willing. And at Paris, in the centre, it is as we saw; and in La Vendee, South-West, it is as we saw; and Sardinia is in the South-East, and Spain is in the South, and Clairfait with Austria and sieged Thionville is in the North; – and all France leaps distracted, like the winnowed Sahara waltzing in sand-colonnades! More desperate posture no country ever stood in. A country, one would say, which the Majesty of Prussia (if it so pleased him) might partition, and clip in pieces, like a Poland; flinging the remainder to poor Brother Louis, – with directions to keep it quiet, or else we will keep it for him!

Or perhaps the Upper Powers, minded that a new Chapter in Universal History shall begin here and not further on, may have ordered it all otherwise? In that case, Brunswick will not dine in Paris on the set day; nor, indeed, one knows not when! – Verily, amid this wreckage, where poor France seems grinding itself down to dust and bottomless ruin, who knows what miraculous salient-point of Deliverance and New-life may have already come into existence there; and be already working there, though as yet human eye discern it not! On the night of that same twenty-eighth of August, the unpromising Review-day in Sedan, Dumouriez assembles a Council of War at his lodgings there. He spreads out the map of this forlorn war-district: Prussians here, Austrians there; triumphant both, with broad highway, and little hinderance, all the way to Paris; we, scattered helpless, here and here: what to advise? The Generals, strangers to Dumouriez, look blank enough; know not well what to advise, – if it be not retreating, and retreating till our recruits accumulate; till perhaps the chapter of chances turn up some leaf for us; or Paris, at all events, be sacked at the latest day possible. The Many-counselled, who 'has not closed an eye for three nights,' listens with little speech to these long cheerless speeches; merely watching the speaker that he may know him; then wishes them all good-night; – but beckons a certain young Thouvenot, the fire of whose looks had pleased him, to wait a moment. Thouvenot waits: Voila, says Polymetis, pointing to the map! That is the Forest of Argonne, that long stripe of rocky Mountain and wild Wood; forty miles long; with but five, or say even three practicable Passes through it: this, for they have forgotten it, might one not still seize, though Clairfait sits so nigh? Once seized; – the Champagne called the Hungry (or worse, Champagne Pouilleuse) on their side of it; the fat Three Bishoprics, and willing France, on ours; and the Equinox-rains not far; – this Argonne 'might be the Thermopylae of France!'

O brisk Dumouriez Polymetis with thy teeming head, may the gods grant it! – Polymetis, at any rate, folds his map together, and flings himself on bed; resolved to try, on the morrow morning. With astucity, with swiftness, with audacity! One had need to be a lion-fox, and have luck on one's side.

SEPTEMBER IN PARIS.

At Paris, by lying Rumour which proved prophetic and veridical, the fall of Verdun was known some hours before it happened. It is Sunday the second of September; handiwork

hinders not the speculations of the mind. Verdun gone
(though some still deny it); the Prussians in full march,
with gallows-ropes, with fire and faggot! Thirty thousand
Aristocrats within our own walls; and but the merest quarter-
tithe of them yet put in Prison! Nay there goes a word
that even these will revolt. Sieur Jean Julien, wagoner of
Vaugirard, being set in the Pillory last Friday, took all at once
to crying, That he would be well revenged ere long; that the
King's Friends in Prison would burst out; force the Temple,
set the King on horseback; and, joined by the unimprisoned,
ride roughshod over us all. This the unfortunate wagoner of
Vaugirard did bawl, at the top of his lungs: when snatched off
to the Townhall, he persisted in it, still bawling; yesternight,
when they guillotined him, he died with the froth of it on
his lips. For a man's mind, padlocked to the Pillory, may go
mad; and all men's minds may go mad; and 'believe him,' as
the frenetic will do, 'because it is impossible.'

So that apparently the knot of the crisis, and last agony
of France is come? Make front to this, thou Improvised
Commune, strong Danton, whatsoever man is strong!
Readers can judge whether the Flag of Country in Danger
flapped soothing or distractively on the souls of men, that
day.

But the Improvised Commune, but strong Danton is
not wanting, each after his kind. Huge Placards are getting
plastered to the walls; at two o'clock the stormbell shall
be sounded, the alarm-cannon fired; all Paris shall rush to
the Champ-de-Mars, and have itself enrolled. Unarmed,
truly, and undrilled; but desperate, in the strength of frenzy.
Haste, ye men; ye very women, offer to mount guard and
shoulder the brown musket: weak clucking-hens, in a

state of desperation, will fly at the muzzle of the mastiff, and even conquer him, – by vehemence of character! Terror itself, when once grown transcendental, becomes a kind of courage; as frost sufficiently intense, according to Poet Milton, will burn. – Danton, the other night, in the Legislative Committee of General Defence, when the other Ministers and Legislators had all opined, said, It would not do to quit Paris, and fly to Saumur; that they must abide by Paris; and take such attitude as would put their enemies in fear, – faire peur; a word of his which has been often repeated, and reprinted – in italics.

At two of the clock, Beaurepaire, as we saw, has shot himself at Verdun; and over Europe, mortals are going in for afternoon sermon. But at Paris, all steeples are clangouring not for sermon; the alarm-gun booming from minute to minute; Champ-de-Mars and Fatherland's Altar boiling with desperate terror-courage: what a miserere going up to Heaven from this once Capital of the Most Christian King! The Legislative sits in alternate awe and effervescence; Vergniaud proposing that Twelve shall go and dig personally on Montmartre; which is decreed by acclaim.

But better than digging personally with acclaim, see Danton enter; – the black brows clouded, the colossus-figure tramping heavy; grim energy looking from all features of the rugged man! Strong is that grim Son of France, and Son of Earth; a Reality and not a Formula he too; and surely now if ever, being hurled low enough, it is on the Earth and on Realities that he rests. "Legislators!" so speaks the stentor-voice, as the Newspapers yet preserve it for us, "it is not the alarm-cannon that you hear: it is the pas-de-charge against our enemies. To conquer them, to hurl them back,

what do we require? Il nous faut de l'audace, et encore de
l'audace, et toujours de l'audace, To dare, and again to dare,
and without end to dare!" (Moniteur in Hist. Parl. xvii. 347.)
– Right so, thou brawny Titan; there is nothing left for thee
but that. Old men, who heard it, will still tell you how the
reverberating voice made all hearts swell, in that moment;
and braced them to the sticking-place; and thrilled abroad
over France, like electric virtue, as a word spoken in season.

But the Commune, enrolling in the Champ-de-Mars? But
the Committee of Watchfulness, become now Committee
of Public Salvation; whose conscience is Marat? The
Commune enrolling enrolls many; provides Tents for them
in that Mars'-Field, that they may march with dawn on the
morrow: praise to this part of the Commune! To Marat
and the Committee of Watchfulness not praise; – not even
blame, such as could be meted out in these insufficient
dialects of ours; expressive silence rather! Lone Marat, the
man forbid, meditating long in his Cellars of refuge, on his
Stylites Pillar, could see salvation in one thing only: in the fall
of 'two hundred and sixty thousand Aristocrat heads.' With
so many score of Naples Bravoes, each a dirk in his right-
hand, a muff on his left, he would traverse France, and do
it. But the world laughed, mocking the severe-benevolence
of a People's-Friend; and his idea could not become an
action, but only a fixed-idea. Lo, now, however, he has come
down from his Stylites Pillar, to a Tribune particuliere; here
now, without the dirks, without the muffs at least, were it
not grown possible, – now in the knot of the crisis, when
salvation or destruction hangs in the hour!

The Ice-Tower of Avignon was noised of sufficiently, and
lives in all memories; but the authors were not punished: nay

we saw Jourdan Coupe-tete, borne on men's shoulders, like a copper Portent, 'traversing the cities of the South.' – What phantasms, squalid-horrid, shaking their dirk and muff, may dance through the brain of a Marat, in this dizzy pealing of tocsin-miserere, and universal frenzy, seek not to guess, O Reader! Nor what the cruel Billaud 'in his short brown coat was thinking;' nor Sergent, not yet Agate-Sergent; nor Panis the confident of Danton; – nor, in a word, how gloomy Orcus does breed in her gloomy womb, and fashion her monsters, and prodigies of Events, which thou seest her visibly bear! Terror is on these streets of Paris; terror and rage, tears and frenzy: tocsin-miserere pealing through the air; fierce desperation rushing to battle; mothers, with streaming eyes and wild hearts, sending forth their sons to die. 'Carriage-horses are seized by the bridle,' that they may draw cannon; 'the traces cut, the carriages left standing.' In such tocsin-miserere, and murky bewilderment of Frenzy, are not Murder, Ate, and all Furies near at hand? On slight hint, who knows on how slight, may not Murder come; and, with her snaky-sparkling hand, illuminate this murk!

How it was and went, what part might be premeditated, what was improvised and accidental, man will never know, till the great Day of Judgment make it known. But with a Marat for keeper of the Sovereign's Conscience – And we know what the ultima ratio of Sovereigns, when they are driven to it, is! In this Paris there are as many wicked men, say a hundred or more, as exist in all the Earth: to be hired, and set on; to set on, of their own accord, unhired. – And yet we will remark that premeditation itself is not performance, is not surety of performance; that it is perhaps, at most, surety of letting whosoever wills perform. From the purpose of crime to the act of crime there is an abyss; wonderful to think of. The finger lies on the pistol; but the man is not yet a murderer: nay, his whole nature staggering at such consummation, is there not a confused pause rather, – one last instant of possibility for him? Not yet a murderer; it is at the mercy of light trifles whether the most fixed idea may not yet become unfixed. One slight twitch of a muscle, the death flash bursts; and he is it, and will for Eternity be it; – and Earth has become a penal Tartarus for him; his horizon girdled now not with golden hope, but with red flames of remorse; voices from the depths of Nature sounding, Wo, wo on him!

Of such stuff are we all made; on such powder-mines of bottomless guilt and criminality, 'if God restrained not; as is well said, – does the purest of us walk. There are depths in man that go the length of lowest Hell, as there are heights that reach highest Heaven; – for are not both Heaven and Hell made out of him, made by him, everlasting Miracle and Mystery as he is? – But looking on this Champ-de-Mars, with its tent-buildings, and frantic enrolments; on this murky-simmering Paris, with its crammed Prisons (supposed about to burst), with its tocsin-miserere, its mothers' tears, and soldiers' farewell shoutings, – the pious soul might have prayed, that day, that God's grace would restrain, and greatly restrain; lest on slight hest or hint, Madness, Horror and Murder rose, and this Sabbath-day of September became a Day black in the Annals of Men. –

The tocsin is pealing its loudest, the clocks inaudibly striking Three, when poor Abbe Sicard, with some thirty other Nonjurant Priests, in six carriages, fare along the streets, from their preliminary House of Detention at the

119

Townhall, westward towards the Prison of the Abbaye. Carriages enough stand deserted on the streets; these six move on, – through angry multitudes, cursing as they move. Accursed Aristocrat Tartuffes, this is the pass ye have brought us to! And now ye will break the Prisons, and set Capet Veto on horseback to ride over us? Out upon you, Priests of Beelzebub and Moloch; of Tartuffery, Mammon, and the Prussian Gallows, – which ye name Mother-Church and God! Such reproaches have the poor Nonjurants to endure, and worse; spoken in on them by frantic Patriots, who mount even on the carriage-steps; the very Guards hardly refraining. Pull up your carriage-blinds! – No! answers Patriotism, clapping its horny paw on the carriage blind, and crushing it down again. Patience in oppression has limits: we are close on the Abbaye, it has lasted long: a poor Nonjurant, of quicker temper, smites the horny paw with his cane; nay, finding solacement in it, smites the unkempt head, sharply and again more sharply, twice over, – seen clearly of us and of the world. It is the last that we see clearly. Alas, next moment, the carriages are locked and blocked in endless raging tumults; in yells deaf to the cry for mercy, which answer the cry for mercy with sabre-thrusts through the heart. The thirty Priests are torn out, are massacred about the Prison-Gate, one after one, – only the poor Abbe Sicard, whom one Moton a watchmaker, knowing him, heroically tried to save, and secrete in the Prison, escapes to tell; – and it is Night and Orcus, and Murder's snaky-sparkling head has risen in the murk! –

From Sunday afternoon (exclusive of intervals, and pauses not final) till Thursday evening, there follow consecutively a Hundred Hours. Which hundred hours are to be reckoned with the hours of the Bartholomew Butchery, of the Armagnac Massacres, Sicilian Vespers, or whatsoever is savagest in the annals of this world. Horrible the hour when man's soul, in its paroxysm, spurns asunder the barriers and rules; and shews what dens and depths are in it! For Night and Orcus, as we say, as was long prophesied, have burst forth, here in this Paris, from their subterranean imprisonment: hideous, dim, confused; which it is painful to look on; and yet which cannot, and indeed which should not, be forgotten.

The Reader, who looks earnestly through this dim Phantasmagory of the Pit, will discern few fixed certain objects; and yet still a few. He will observe, in this Abbaye Prison, the sudden massacre of the Priests being once over, a strange Court of Justice, or call it Court of Revenge and Wild-Justice, swiftly fashion itself, and take seat round a table, with the Prison-Registers spread before it; – Stanislas Maillard, Bastille-hero, famed Leader of the Menads, presiding. O Stanislas, one hoped to meet thee elsewhere than here; thou shifty Riding-Usher, with an inkling of Law! This work also thou hadst to do; and then – to depart for ever from our eyes. At La Force, at the Chatelet, the Conciergerie, the like Court forms itself, with the like accompaniments: the thing that one man does other men can do. There are some Seven Prisons in Paris, full of Aristocrats with conspiracies; – nay not even Bicetre and Salpetriere shall escape, with their Forgers of Assignats: and there are seventy times seven hundred Patriot hearts in a state of frenzy. Scoundrel hearts also there are; as perfect, say, as the Earth holds, – if such are needed. To whom, in this mood, law is as no-law; and killing, by what name soever called, is but work to be done.

So sit these sudden Courts of Wild-Justice, with the Prison-Registers before them; unwonted wild tumult howling all round: the Prisoners in dread expectancy within. Swift: a name is called; bolts jingle, a Prisoner is there. A few questions are put; swiftly this sudden Jury decides: Royalist Plotter or not? Clearly not; in that case, Let the Prisoner be enlarged With Vive la Nation. Probably yea; then still, Let the Prisoner be enlarged, but without Vive la Nation; or else it may run, Let the prisoner be conducted to La Force. At La Force again their formula is, Let the Prisoner be conducted to the Abbaye. – "To La Force then!" Volunteer bailiffs seize the doomed man; he is at the outer gate; 'enlarged,' or 'conducted,' – not into La Force, but into a howling sea; forth, under an arch of wild sabres, axes and pikes; and sinks, hewn asunder. And another sinks, and another; and there forms itself a piled heap of corpses, and the kennels begin to run red. Fancy the yells of these men, their faces of sweat and blood; the crueller shrieks of these women, for there are women too; and a fellow-mortal hurled naked into it all! Jourgniac de Saint Meard has seen battle, has seen an effervescent Regiment du Roi in mutiny; but the bravest heart may quail at this. The Swiss Prisoners, remnants of the Tenth of August, 'clasped each other spasmodically,' and hung back; grey veterans crying: "Mercy Messieurs; ah, mercy!" But there was no mercy. Suddenly, however, one of these men steps forward. He had a blue frock coat; he seemed to be about thirty, his stature was above common, his look noble and martial. "I go first," said he, "since it must be so: adieu!" Then dashing his hat sharply behind him: "Which way?" cried he to the Brigands: "Shew it me, then." They open the folding gate; he is announced to the multitude. He stands a moment motionless; then plunges forth among the pikes, and dies of a thousand wounds.'

Man after man is cut down; the sabres need sharpening, the killers refresh themselves from wine jugs. Onward and onward goes the butchery; the loud yells wearying down into bass growls. A sombre-faced, shifting multitude looks on; in dull approval, or dull disapproval; in dull recognition that it is Necessity. 'An Anglais in drab greatcoat' was seen, or seemed to be seen, serving liquor from his own dram-bottle; – for what purpose, 'if not set on by Pitt,' Satan and himself know best! Witty Dr. Moore grew sick on approaching, and turned into another street. Quick enough goes this Jury-Court; and rigorous. The brave are not spared, nor the beautiful, nor the weak. Old M. de Montmorin, the Minister's Brother, was acquitted by the Tribunal of the Seventeenth; and conducted back, elbowed by howling galleries; but is not acquitted here. Princess de Lamballe has lain down on bed: "Madame, you are to be removed to the Abbaye." "I do not wish to remove; I am well enough here." There is a need-be for removing. She will arrange her dress a little, then; rude voices answer, "You have not far to go." She too is led to the hell-gate; a manifest Queen's-Friend. She shivers back, at the sight of bloody sabres; but there is no return: Onwards! That fair hindhead is cleft with the axe; the neck is severed. That fair body is cut in fragments; with indignities, and obscene horrors of moustachio grands-levres, which human nature would fain find incredible, – which shall be read in the original language only. She was beautiful, she was good, she had known no happiness. Young hearts, generation after generation, will think with themselves: O worthy of worship, thou king-descended, god-descended and poor sister-woman! why was not I there; and some Sword Balmung, or Thor's Hammer in my hand? Her head is fixed on a pike; paraded under the windows of the Temple; that a still more hated, a Marie-Antoinette, may see. One Municipal, in the Temple with the Royal Prisoners at the moment, said, "Look out." Another eagerly whispered, "Do not look." The circuit of the Temple is guarded, in these hours, by a long stretched tricolor riband: terror enters, and the clangour of infinite tumult: hitherto not regicide, though that too may come.

But it is more edifying to note what thrillings of affection, what fragments of wild virtues turn up, in this shaking asunder of man's existence, for of these too there is a proportion. Note old Marquis Cazotte: he is doomed to die; but his young Daughter clasps him in her arms, with an inspiration of eloquence, with a love which is stronger than very death; the heart of the killers themselves is touched by it; the old man is spared. Yet he was guilty, if plotting for his King is guilt: in ten days more, a Court of Law condemned him, and he had to die elsewhere; bequeathing his Daughter a lock of his old grey hair. Or note old M. de Sombreuil, who also had a Daughter: – My Father is not an Aristocrat; O good gentlemen, I will swear it, and testify it, and in all ways prove it; we are not; we hate Aristocrats! "Wilt thou drink Aristocrats' blood?" The man lifts blood (if universal Rumour can be credited. "This Sombreuil is innocent then!" Yes indeed, – and now note, most of all, how the bloody pikes, at this news, do rattle to the ground; and the tiger-yells become bursts of jubilee over a brother saved; and the old man and his daughter are clasped to bloody bosoms, with hot tears, and borne home in triumph of Vive la Nation, the killers refusing even money! Does it seem strange, this temper of theirs? It seems very certain, well proved by Royalist testimony in other instances; and very significant.

THE CIRCULAR.

This is the September Massacre, otherwise called 'Severe Justice of the People.' These are the Septemberers (Septembriseurs); a name of some note and lucency, – but lucency of the Nether-fire sort; very different from that of our Bastille Heroes, who shone, disputable by no Friend of Freedom, as in heavenly light-radiance: to such phasis of the business have we advanced since then! The numbers massacred are, in Historical fantasy, 'between two and three thousand;' or indeed they are 'upwards of six thousand,' for Peltier (in vision) saw them massacring the very patients of the Bicetre Madhouse 'with grape-shot;' nay finally they are 'twelve thousand' and odd hundreds, – not more than that. In Arithmetical ciphers, and Lists drawn up by accurate Advocate Maton, the number, including two hundred and two priests, three 'persons unknown,' and 'one thief killed at the Bernardins,' is, as above hinted, a Thousand and Eighty-nine, – no less than that.

A thousand and eighty-nine lie dead, 'two hundred and sixty heaped carcasses on the Pont au Change' itself; – among which, Robespierre pleading afterwards will 'nearly weep' to reflect that there was said to be one slain innocent. One; not two, O thou seagreen Incorruptible? If so, Themis Sansculotte must be lucky; for she was brief! – In the dim Registers of the Townhall, which are preserved to this day, men read, with a certain sickness of heart, items and entries not usual in Town Books: 'To workers employed in preserving the salubrity of the air in the Prisons, and persons 'who presided over these dangerous operations,' so much, – in various items, nearly seven hundred pounds sterling. To carters employed to 'the

Burying-grounds of Clamart, Montrouge, and Vaugirard,'
at so much a journey, per cart; this also is an entry. Then
so many francs and odd sous 'for the necessary quantity of
quick-lime!' Carts go along the streets; full of stript human
corpses, thrown pellmell; limbs sticking up: – seest thou
that cold Hand sticking up, through the heaped embrace
of brother corpses, in its yellow paleness, in its cold rigour;
the palm opened towards Heaven, as if in dumb prayer, in
expostulation de profundis, Take pity on the Sons of Men!
– Mercier saw it, as he walked down 'the Rue Saint-Jacques
from Montrouge, on the morrow of the Massacres:' but
not a Hand; it was a Foot, – which he reckons still more
significant, one understands not well why. Or was it as the
Foot of one spurning Heaven? Rushing, like a wild diver,
in disgust and despair, towards the depths of Annihilation?
Even there shall His hand find thee, and His right-hand hold
thee, – surely for right not for wrong, for good not evil! 'I
saw that Foot,' says Mercier; 'I shall know it again at the
great Day of Judgment, when the Eternal, throned on his
thunders, shall judge both Kings and Septemberers.'

That a shriek of inarticulate horror rose over this thing,
not only from French Aristocrats and Moderates, but from
all Europe, and has prolonged itself to the present day, was
most natural and right. The thing lay done, irrevocable; a
thing to be counted besides some other things, which lie
very black in our Earth's Annals, yet which will not erase
therefrom. For man, as was remarked, has transcendentalisms
in him; standing, as he does, poor creature, every way 'in the
confluence of Infinitudes;' a mystery to himself and others:
in the centre of two Eternities, of three Immensities, – in the
intersection of primeval Light with the everlasting dark! Thus

have there been, especially by vehement tempers reduced to a state of desperation, very miserable things done. Sicilian Vespers, and 'eight thousand slaughtered in two hours,' are a known thing. Kings themselves, not in desperation, but only in difficulty, have sat hatching, for year and day (nay De Thou says, for seven years), their Bartholomew Business; and then, at the right moment, also on an Autumn Sunday, this very Bell (they say it is the identical metal) of St. Germain l'Auxerrois was set a-pealing – with effect. (9th to 13th September, 1572.) Nay the same black boulder-stones of these Paris Prisons have seen Prison-massacres before now; men massacring countrymen, Burgundies massacring Armagnacs, whom they had suddenly imprisoned, till as now there are piled heaps of carcasses, and the streets ran red; – the Mayor Petion of the time speaking the austere language of the law, and answered by the Killers, in old French (it is some four hundred years old): "Maugre bieu, Sire, – Sir, God's malison on your justice, your pity, your right reason. Cursed be of God whoso shall have pity on these false traitorous Armagnacs, English; dogs they are; they have destroyed us, wasted this realm of France, and sold it to the English." And so they slay, and fling aside the slain, to the extent of 'fifteen hundred and eighteen, among whom are found four Bishops of false and damnable counsel, and two Presidents of Parlement.' For though it is not Satan's world this that we live in, Satan always has his place in it (underground properly); and from time to time bursts up. Well may mankind shriek, inarticulately anathematising as they can. There are actions of such emphasis that no shrieking can be too emphatic for them. Shriek ye; acted have they.

To shriek, we say, when certain things are acted, is proper and unavoidable. Nevertheless, articulate speech, not shrieking, is the faculty of man: when speech is not yet possible, let there be, with the shortest delay, at least – silence. Silence, accordingly, in this forty-fourth year of the business, and eighteen hundred and thirty-sixth of an 'Era called Christian as lucus a non,' is the thing we recommend and practise. Nay, instead of shrieking more, it were perhaps edifying to remark, on the other side, what a singular thing Customs (in Latin, Mores) are; and how fitly the Virtue, Vir-tus, Manhood or Worth, that is in a man, is called his Morality, or Customariness. Fell Slaughter, one the most authentic products of the Pit you would say, once give it Customs, becomes War, with Laws of War; and is Customary and Moral enough; and red individuals carry the tools of it girt round their haunches, not without an air of pride, – which do thou nowise blame. While, see! so long as it is but dressed in hodden or russet; and Revolution, less frequent than War, has not yet got its Laws of Revolution, but the hodden or russet individuals are Uncustomary – O shrieking beloved brother blockheads of Mankind, let us close those wide mouths of ours; let us cease shrieking, and begin considering!

THE DELIBERATIVE.

In truth, it is very singular to see how this mercurial French People plunges suddenly from Vive le Roi to Vive la Republique; and goes simmering and dancing; shaking off daily (so to speak), and trampling into the dust, its old social garnitures, ways of thinking, rules of existing; and cheerfully dances towards the Ruleless, Unknown, with such hope in its heart, and nothing but Freedom, Equality and Brotherhood in its mouth. Is it two centuries, or is it only two years, since all France roared simultaneously to the welkin, bursting forth into sound and smoke at its Feast of Pikes, "Live the Restorer of French Liberty?" Three short years ago there was still Versailles and an Oeil-de-Boeuf: now there is that watched Circuit of the Temple, girt with dragon-eyed Municipals, where, as in its final limbo, Royalty lies extinct. In the year 1789, Constituent Deputy Barrere 'wept,' in his Break-of-Day Newspaper, at sight of a reconciled King Louis; and now in 1792, Convention Deputy Barrere, perfectly tearless, may be considering, whether the reconciled King Louis shall be guillotined or not.

DISCROWNED.

King Louis, now King and Majesty to his own family alone, in their own Prison Apartment alone, has been Louis Capet and the Traitor Veto with the rest of France. Shut in his Circuit of the Temple, he has heard and seen the loud whirl of things; yells of September Massacres, Brunswick war-thunders dying off in disaster and discomfiture; he passive, a spectator merely; – waiting whither it would please to whirl with him. From the neighbouring windows, the curious, not without pity, might see him walk daily, at a certain hour, in the Temple Garden, with his Queen, Sister and two Children, all that now belongs to him in this Earth. Quietly he walks and waits; for he is not of lively feelings, and is of a devout heart. The wearied Irresolute has, at least, no need of resolving now. His daily meals, lessons to his Son, daily walk in the Garden, daily game at ombre or drafts, fill up the day: the morrow will provide for itself.

The morrow indeed; and yet How? Louis asks, How? France, with perhaps still more solicitude, asks, How? A King dethroned by insurrection is verily not easy to dispose of. Keep him prisoner, he is a secret centre for the Disaffected, for endless plots, attempts and hopes of theirs. Banish him, he is an open centre for them; his royal war-standard, with what of divinity it has, unrolls itself, summoning the world. Put him to death? A cruel questionable extremity that too: and yet the likeliest in these extreme circumstances, of insurrectionary men, whose own life and death lies staked: accordingly it is said, from the last step of the throne to the first of the scaffold there is short distance.

But, on the whole, we will remark here that this business of Louis looks altogether different now, as seen over Seas and at the distance of forty-four years, than it looked then, in France, and struggling, confused all round one! For indeed it is a most lying thing that same Past Tense always: so beautiful, sad, almost Elysian-sacred, 'in the moonlight of Memory,' it seems; and seems only. For observe: always, one most important element is surreptitiously (we not noticing it) withdrawn from the Past Time: the haggard element of Fear! Not there does Fear dwell, nor Uncertainty, nor Anxiety; but it dwells here; haunting us, tracking us; running like an accursed ground-discord through all the music-tones of our Existence; – making the Tense a mere Present one! Just so is it with this of Louis. Why smite the fallen? asks Magnanimity, out of danger now. He is fallen so low this once-high man; no criminal nor traitor, how far from it; but the unhappiest of Human Solecisms: whom if abstract Justice had to pronounce upon, she might well become concrete Pity, and pronounce only sobs and dismissal!

So argues retrospective Magnanimity: but Pusillanimity, present, prospective? Reader, thou hast never lived, for months, under the rustle of Prussian gallows-ropes; never wert thou portion of a National Sahara-waltz, Twenty-five millions running distracted to fight Brunswick! Knights Errant themselves, when they conquered Giants, usually slew the Giants: quarter was only for other Knights Errant, who knew courtesy and the laws of battle. The French Nation, in simultaneous, desperate dead-pull, and as if by miracle of madness, has pulled down the most dread Goliath, huge with the growth of ten centuries; and cannot believe, though his giant bulk, covering acres, lies prostrate, bound with peg and packthread, that he will not rise again, man-devouring; that the victory is not partly a dream. Terror has its scepticism; miraculous victory its rage of vengeance. Then as to criminalty, is the prostrated Giant, who will devour us if he rise, an innocent Giant? Curate Gregoire, who indeed is now Constitutional Bishop Gregoire, asserts, in the heat of eloquence, that Kingship by the very nature of it is a crime capital; that Kings' Houses are as wild-beasts' dens. Lastly consider this: that there is on record a Trial of Charles First! This printed Trial of Charles First is sold and read every where at present: Quelle spectacle! Thus did the English People judge their Tyrant, and become the first of Free Peoples: which feat, by the grace of Destiny, may not France now rival? Scepticism of terror, rage of miraculous victory, sublime spectacle to the universe, – all things point one fatal way.

THE THREE VOTINGS.

Is Louis Capet guilty of conspiring against Liberty? Shall our Sentence be itself final, or need ratifying by Appeal to the People? If guilty, what Punishment? This is the form agreed to, after uproar and 'several hours of tumultuous indecision:' these are the Three successive Questions, whereon the Convention shall now pronounce. Paris floods round their Hall; multitudinous, many sounding. Europe and all Nations listen for their answer. Deputy after Deputy shall answer to his name: Guilty or Not guilty?

As to the Guilt, there is, as above hinted, no doubt in the mind of Patriot man. Overwhelming majority pronounces Guilt; the unanimous Convention votes for Guilt, only some feeble twenty-eight voting not Innocence, but refusing to vote at all. Neither does the Second Question prove doubtful, whatever the Girondins might calculate. Would not Appeal to the People be another name for civil war? Majority of two to one answers that there shall be no Appeal: this also is settled. Loud Patriotism, now at ten o'clock, may hush itself for the night; and retire to its bed not without hope. Tuesday has gone well. On the morrow comes, What Punishment? On the morrow is the tug of war.

Consider therefore if, on this Wednesday morning, there is an affluence of Patriotism; if Paris stands a-tiptoe, and all Deputies are at their post! Seven Hundred and Forty-nine honourable Deputies; only some twenty absent on mission, Duchatel and some seven others absent by sickness. Meanwhile expectant Patriotism and Paris standing a-tiptoe, have need of patience. For this Wednesday again passes in debate and effervescence; Girondins proposing that a 'majority of three-fourths' shall be required; Patriots fiercely resisting them. Danton, who has just got back from mission in the Netherlands, does obtain 'order of the day' on this Girondin proposal; nay he obtains further that we decide sans desemparer, in Permanent-session, till we have done.

And so, finally, at eight in the evening this Third stupendous Voting, by roll-call or appel nominal, does begin. What Punishment? Girondins undecided, Patriots decided, men afraid of Royalty, men afraid of Anarchy, must answer here and now. Infinite Patriotism, dusky in the lamp-light, floods all corridors, crowds all galleries, sternly waiting to hear. Shrill-sounding Ushers summon you by Name and Department; you must rise to the Tribune and say.

Eye-witnesses have represented this scene of the Third Voting, and of the votings that grew out of it; a scene protracted, like to be endless, lasting, with few brief intervals, from Wednesday till Sunday morning, – as one of the strangest seen in the Revolution. Long night wears itself into day, morning's paleness is spread over all faces; and again the wintry shadows sink, and the dim lamps are lit: but through day and night and the vicissitude of hours, Member after Member is mounting continually those Tribune-steps; pausing aloft there, in the clearer upper light, to speak his Fate-word; then diving down into the dusk and throng again. Like Phantoms in the hour of midnight; most spectral, pandemonial! Never did President Vergniaud, or any terrestrial President, superintend the like. A King's Life, and so much else that depends thereon, hangs trembling in the balance. Man after man mounts; the buzz hushes itself till he have spoken: Death; Banishment: Imprisonment till the Peace. Many say, Death; with what cautious well-studied phrases and paragraphs they could devise, of explanation, of enforcement, of faint recommendation to mercy. Many too say, Banishment; something short of Death. The balance trembles, none can yet guess whitherward. Whereat anxious Patriotism bellows; irrepressible by Ushers.

The poor Girondins, many of them, under such fierce bellowing of Patriotism, say Death; justifying, motivant, that most miserable word of theirs by some brief casuistry and jesuitry. Vergniaud himself says, Death; justifying by jesuitry. Rich Lepelletier Saint-Fargeau had been of the Noblesse, and then of the Patriot Left Side, in the Constituent; and had argued and reported, there and elsewhere, not a little, against Capital Punishment: nevertheless he now says, Death; a word which may cost him dear. Manuel did surely rank with the Decided in August last; but he has been sinking and backsliding ever since September, and the scenes of September. In this Convention, above all, no word he could speak would find favour; he says now, Banishment; and in mute wrath quits the place for ever, – much hustled in the corridors. Philippe Egalite votes in his soul and conscience, Death, at the sound of which, and of whom, even Patriotism shakes its head; and there runs a groan and shudder through this Hall of Doom. Robespierre's vote cannot be doubtful; his speech is long. Men see the figure of shrill Sieyes ascend; hardly pausing, passing merely, this figure says, "La Mort sans phrase, Death without phrases;" and fares onward and downward. Most spectral, pandemonial!

And yet if the Reader fancy it of a funereal, sorrowful or even grave character, he is far mistaken. 'The Ushers in the Mountain quarter,' says Mercier, 'had become as Box-openers at the Opera;' opening and shutting of Galleries for privileged

persons, for 'd'Orleans Egalite's mistresses,' or other high-dizened women of condition, rustling with laces and tricolor.
Gallant Deputies pass and repass thitherward, treating them
with ices, refreshments and small-talk; the high-dizened heads
beck responsive; some have their card and pin, pricking down
the Ayes and Noes, as at a game of Rouge-et-Noir. Further
aloft reigns Mere Duchesse with her unrouged Amazons; she
cannot be prevented making long Hahas, when the vote is
not La Mort. In these Galleries there is refection, drinking of
wine and brandy 'as in open tavern, en pleine tabagie.' Betting
goes on in all coffeehouses of the neighbourhood. But within
doors, fatigue, impatience, uttermost weariness sits now on
all visages; lighted up only from time to time, by turns of the
game. Members have fallen asleep; Ushers come and awaken
them to vote: other Members calculate whether they shall not
have time to run and dine. Figures rise, like phantoms, pale in
the dusky lamp-light; utter from this Tribune, only one word:
Death. 'Tout est optique,' says Mercier, 'the world is all an
optical shadow.' Deep in the Thursday night, when the Voting is done, and Secretaries are summing it up, sick Duchatel,
more spectral than another, comes borne on a chair, wrapt in
blankets, 'in nightgown and nightcap,' to vote for Mercy: one
vote it is thought may turn the scale.

Ah no! In profoundest silence, President Vergniaud, with
a voice full of sorrow, has to say: "I declare, in the name
of the Convention, that the Punishment it pronounces on
Louis Capet is that of Death." Death by a small majority
of Fifty-three. Nay, if we deduct from the one side, and
add to the other, a certain Twenty-six, who said Death but
coupled some faintest ineffectual surmise of mercy with it,
the majority will be but One.

Death is the sentence: but its execution? It is not executed yet! Scarcely is the vote declared when Louis's Three Advocates enter; with Protest in his name, with demand for Delay, for Appeal to the People. For this do Deseze and Tronchet plead, with brief eloquence: brave old Malesherbes pleads for it with eloquent want of eloquence, in broken sentences, in embarrassment and sobs; that brave time-honoured face, with its grey strength, its broad sagacity and honesty, is mastered with emotion, melts into dumb tears. They reject the Appeal to the People; that having been already settled. But as to the Delay, what they call Sursis, it shall be considered; shall be voted for to-morrow: at present we adjourn. Whereupon Patriotism 'hisses' from the Mountain: but a 'tyrannical majority' has so decided, and adjourns.

There is still this fourth Vote then, growls indignant Patriotism: – this vote, and who knows what other votes, and adjournments of voting; and the whole matter still hovering hypothetical! And at every new vote those Jesuit Girondins, even they who voted for Death, would so fain find a loophole! Patriotism must watch and rage. Tyrannical adjournments there have been; one, and now another at midnight on plea of fatigue, – all Friday wasted in hesitation and higgling; in re-counting of the votes, which are found correct as they stood! Patriotism bays fiercer than ever; Patriotism, by long-watching, has become red-eyed, almost rabid.

"Delay: yes or no?" men do vote it finally, all Saturday, all day and night. Men's nerves are worn out, men's hearts are desperate; now it shall end. Vergniaud, spite of the baying, ventures to say Yes, Delay; though he had voted Death. Philippe Egalite says, in his soul and conscience, No. The next Member mounting: "Since Philippe says No, I for my part say Yes, Moi je dis Oui." The balance still trembles. Till finally, at three o'clock on Sunday morning, we have: No Delay, by a majority of Seventy; Death within four-and-twenty hours!

PLACE DE LA REVOLUTION.

As the clocks strike ten, behold the Place de la Revolution, once Place de Louis Quinze: the Guillotine, mounted near the old Pedestal where once stood the Statue of that Louis! Far round, all bristles with cannons and armed men: spectators crowding in the rear; d'Orleans Egalite there in cabriolet. Swift messengers, hoquetons, speed to the Townhall, every three minutes: near by is the Convention sitting, – vengeful for Lepelletier. Heedless of all, Louis reads his Prayers of the Dying; not till five minutes yet has he finished; then the Carriage opens. What temper he is in? Ten different witnesses will give ten different accounts of it. He is in the collision of all tempers; arrived now at the black Mahlstrom and descent of Death: in sorrow, in indignation, in resignation struggling to be resigned. "Take care of M. Edgeworth," he straitly charges the Lieutenant who is sitting with them: then they two descend.

The drums are beating: "Taisez-vous, Silence!" he cries 'in a terrible voice, d'une voix terrible.' He mounts the scaffold, not without delay; he is in puce coat, breeches of grey, white stockings. He strips off the coat; stands disclosed in a sleeve-waistcoat of white flannel. The Executioners approach to bind him: he spurns, resists; Abbe Edgeworth has to remind him how the Saviour, in whom men trust, submitted to be bound. His hands are tied, his head bare; the fatal moment is come. He advances to the edge of the Scaffold, 'his face very red,' and says: "Frenchmen, I die innocent: it is from the Scaffold and near appearing before God that I tell you so. I pardon my enemies; I desire that France – " A General on horseback, Santerre or another, prances out with uplifted hand: "Tambours!" The drums drown the voice. "Executioners do your duty!" The Executioners, desperate lest themselves be murdered (for Santerre and his Armed Ranks will strike, if they do not), seize the hapless Louis: six of them desperate, him singly desperate, struggling there; and bind him to their plank. Abbe Edgeworth, stooping, bespeaks him: "Son of Saint Louis, ascend to Heaven." The Axe clanks down; a King's Life is shorn away. It is Monday the 21st of January 1793. He was aged Thirty-eight years four months and twenty-eight days.

Executioner Samson shews the Head: fierce shout of Vive la Republique rises, and swells; caps raised on bayonets, hats waving: students of the College of Four Nations take it up, on the far Quais; fling it over Paris. Orleans drives off in his cabriolet; the Townhall Councillors rub their hands, saying, "It is done, It is done." There is dipping of handkerchiefs, of pike-points in the blood. Headsman Samson, though he afterwards denied it, sells locks of the hair: fractions of the puce coat are long after worn in rings. And so, in some half-hour it is done; and the multitude has all departed. Pastrycooks, coffee-sellers, milkmen sing out their trivial quotidian cries: the world wags on, as if this were a common day. In the coffeehouses that evening, says Prudhomme, Patriot shook hands with Patriot in a more cordial manner than usual. Not till some days after, according to Mercier, did public men see what a grave thing it was.

A grave thing it indisputably is; and will have consequences. On the morrow morning, Roland, so long steeped to the lips in disgust and chagrin, sends in his demission. His accounts lie all ready, correct in black-on-white to the uttermost farthing: these he wants but to have audited, that he might retire to remote obscurity to the country and his books. They will never be audited those accounts; he will never get retired thither.

It was on Tuesday that Roland demitted. On Thursday comes Lepelletier St. Fargeau's Funeral, and passage to the Pantheon of Great Men. Notable as the wild pageant of a winter day. The Body is borne aloft, half-bare; the winding sheet disclosing the death-wound: sabre and bloody clothes parade themselves; a 'lugubrious music' wailing harsh naeniae. Oak-crowns shower down from windows; President Vergniaud walks there, with Convention, with Jacobin Society, and all Patriots of every colour, all mourning brotherlike.

Notable also for another thing, this Burial of Lepelletier: it was the last act these men ever did with concert! All Parties and figures of Opinion, that agitate this distracted France and its Convention, now stand, as it were, face to face, and dagger to dagger; the King's Life, round which they all struck and battled, being hurled down. Dumouriez, conquering Holland, growls ominous discontent, at the head of Armies. Men say Dumouriez will have a King; that young d'Orleans Egalite shall be his King. Deputy Fauchet, in the Journal des Amis, curses his day, more bitterly than Job did; invokes the poniards of Regicides, of 'Arras Vipers' or Robespierres, of Pluto Dantons, of horrid Butchers Legendre and Simulacra d'Herbois, to send him swiftly to another world than theirs. This is Te-Deum Fauchet, of the Bastille Victory, of the Cercle Social. Sharp was the death-hail rattling round one's Flag-of-truce, on that Bastille day: but it was soft to such wreckage of high Hope as this; one's New Golden Era going down in leaden dross, and sulphurous black of the Everlasting Darkness!

At home this Killing of a King has divided all friends; and abroad it has united all enemies. Fraternity of Peoples, Revolutionary Propagandism; Atheism, Regicide; total destruction of social order in this world! All Kings, and lovers of Kings, and haters of Anarchy, rank in coalition; as in a war for life. England signifies to Citizen Chauvelin, the Ambassador or rather Ambassador's-Cloak, that he must quit the country in eight days. Ambassador's-Cloak and Ambassador, Chauvelin and Talleyrand, depart accordingly. Talleyrand, implicated in that Iron Press of the Tuileries, thinks it safest to make for America.

England has cast out the Embassy: England declares war, – being shocked principally, it would seem, at the condition of the River Scheldt. Spain declares war; being shocked principally at some other thing; which doubtless the Manifesto indicates. Nay we find it was not England that declared war first, or Spain first; but that France herself declared war first on both of them; a point of immense Parliamentary and Journalistic interest in those days, but which has become of no interest whatever in these. They all declare war. The sword is drawn, the scabbard thrown away. It is even as Danton said, in one of his all-too gigantic figures: "The coalised Kings threaten us; we hurl at their feet, as gage of battle, the Head of a King."

CAUSE AND EFFECT.

Yes, Reader, here is a miracle. Out of that putrescent rubbish of Scepticism, Sensualism, Sentimentalism, hollow Machiavelism, such a Faith has verily risen; flaming in the heart of a People. A whole People, awakening as it were to consciousness in deep misery, believes that it is within reach of a Fraternal Heaven-on-Earth. With longing arms, it struggles to embrace the Unspeakable; cannot embrace it, owing to certain causes. – Seldom do we find that a whole People can be said to have any Faith at all; except in things which it can eat and handle. Whensoever it gets any Faith, its history becomes spirit-stirring, note-worthy. But since the time when steel Europe shook itself simultaneously, at the word of Hermit Peter, and rushed towards the Sepulchre where God had lain, there was no universal impulse of Faith that one could note. Since Protestantism went silent, no Luther's voice, no Zisca's drum any longer proclaiming that God's Truth was not the Devil's Lie; and the last of the Cameronians (Renwick was the name of him; honour to the name of the brave!) sank, shot, on the Castle Hill of Edinburgh, there was no partial impulse of Faith among Nations. Till now, behold, once more this French Nation believes! Herein, we say, in that astonishing Faith of theirs, lies the miracle. It is a Faith undoubtedly of the more prodigious sort, even among Faiths; and will embody itself in prodigies. It is the soul of that world-prodigy named French Revolution; whereat the world still gazes and shudders.

But, for the rest, let no man ask History to explain by cause-and-effect how the business proceeded henceforth. This battle of Mountain and Gironde, and what follows, is the battle of Fanaticisms and Miracles; unsuitable for cause-and-effect. The sound of it, to the mind, is as a hubbub of voices in distraction; little of articulate is to be gathered by long listening and studying; only battle-tumult, shouts of triumph, shrieks of despair. The Mountain has left no Memoirs; the Girondins have left Memoirs, which are too often little other than long-drawn Interjections, of Woe is me and Cursed be ye. So soon as History can philosophically delineate the conflagration of a kindled Fireship, she may try this other task. Here lay the bitumen-stratum, there the brimstone one; so ran the vein of gunpowder, of nitre, terebinth and foul grease: this, were she inquisitive enough, History might partly know. But how they acted and reacted below decks, one fire-stratum playing into the other, by its nature and the art of man, now when all hands ran raging, and the flames lashed high over shrouds and topmast: this let not History attempt.

The Fireship is old France, the old French Form of Life; her creed a Generation of men. Wild are their cries and their ragings there, like spirits tormented in that flame. But, on the whole, are they not gone, O Reader? Their Fireship and they, frightening the world, have sailed away; its flames and its thunders quite away, into the Deep of Time. One thing therefore History will do: pity them all; for it went hard with them all. Not even the seagreen Incorruptible but shall have some pity, some human love, though it takes an effort. And now, so much once thoroughly attained, the rest will become easier. To the eye of equal brotherly pity, innumerable perversions dissipate themselves; exaggerations and execrations fall off, of their own accord. Standing wistfully on the safe shore, we will look, and see, what is of interest to us, what is adapted to us.

SANSCULOTTISM ACCOUTRED.

Let us look, however, at the grand internal Sansculottism and Revolution Prodigy, whether it stirs and waxes: there and not elsewhere hope may still be for France. The Revolution Prodigy, as Decree after Decree issues from the Mountain, like creative fiats, accordant with the nature of the Thing, – is shaping itself rapidly, in these days, into terrific stature and articulation, limb after limb. Last March, 1792, we saw all France flowing in blind terror; shutting town-barriers, boiling pitch for Brigands: happier, this March, that it is a seeing terror; that a creative Mountain exists, which can say fiat! Recruitment proceeds with fierce celerity: nevertheless our Volunteers hesitate to set out, till Treason be punished at home; they do not fly to the frontiers; but only fly hither and thither, demanding and denouncing. The Mountain must speak new fiat, and new fiats.

And does it not speak such? Take, as first example, those Comites Revolutionnaires for the arrestment of Persons Suspect. Revolutionary Committee, of Twelve chosen Patriots, sits in every Township of France; examining the Suspect, seeking arms, making domiciliary visits and arrestments; – caring, generally, that the Republic suffer no detriment. Chosen by universal suffrage, each in its Section, they are a kind of elixir of Jacobinism; some Forty-four Thousand of them awake and alive over France! In Paris and all Towns, every house-door must have the names of the inmates legibly printed on it, 'at a height not exceeding five feet from the ground;' every Citizen must produce his certificatory Carte de Civisme, signed by Section-President; every man be ready to give account of the faith that is in him.

Persons Suspect had as well depart this soil of Liberty! And yet departure too is bad: all Emigrants are declared Traitors, their property become National; they are 'dead in Law,' – save indeed that for our behoof they shall 'live yet fifty years in Law,' and what heritages may fall to them in that time become National too! A mad vitality of Jacobinism, with Forty-four Thousand centres of activity, circulates through all fibres of France.

Very notable also is the Tribunal Extraordinaire: decreed by the Mountain; some Girondins dissenting, for surely such a Court contradicts every formula; – other Girondins assenting, nay co-operating, for do not we all hate Traitors, O ye people of Paris? – Tribunal of the Seventeenth in Autumn last was swift; but this shall be swifter. Five Judges; a standing Jury, which is named from Paris and the Neighbourhood, that there be not delay in naming it: they are subject to no Appeal; to hardly any Law-forms, but must 'get themselves convinced' in all readiest ways; and for security are bound 'to vote audibly;' audibly, in the hearing of a Paris Public. This is the Tribunal Extraordinaire; which, in few months, getting into most lively action, shall be entitled Tribunal Revolutionnaire, as indeed it from the very first has entitled itself: with a Herman or a Dumas for Judge President, with a Fouquier-Tinville for Attorney-General, and a Jury of such as Citizen Leroi, who has surnamed himself Dix-Aout, 'Leroi August-Tenth,' it will become the wonder of the world. Herein has Sansculottism fashioned for itself a Sword of Sharpness: a weapon magical; tempered in the Stygian hell-waters; to the edge of it all armour, and defence of strength or of cunning shall be soft; it shall mow down Lives and Brazen-gates; and the waving of it shed terror through the souls of men.

But speaking of an amorphous Sansculottism taking form, ought we not above all things to specify how the Amorphous gets itself a Head? Without metaphor, this Revolution Government continues hitherto in a very anarchic state. Executive Council of Ministers, Six in number, there is; but they, especially since Roland's retreat, have hardly known whether they were Ministers or not. Convention Committees sit supreme over them; but then each Committee as supreme as the others: Committee of Twenty-one, of Defence, of General Surety; simultaneous or successive, for specific purposes. The Convention alone is all-powerful, – especially if the Commune go with it; but is too numerous for an administrative body. Wherefore, in this perilous quick-whirling condition of the Republic, before the end of March, we obtain our small Comite de Salut Public; as it were, for miscellaneous accidental purposes, requiring despatch; – as it proves, for a sort of universal supervision, and universal subjection. They are to report weekly, these new Committee-men; but to deliberate in secret. Their number is Nine, firm Patriots all, Danton one of them: Renewable every month; – yet why not reelect them if they turn out well? The flower of the matter is that they are but nine; that they sit in secret. An insignificant-looking thing at first, this Committee; but with a principle of growth in it! Forwarded by fortune, by internal Jacobin energy, it will reduce all Committees and the Convention itself to mute obedience, the Six Ministers to Six assiduous Clerks; and work its will on the Earth and under Heaven, for a season. 'A Committee of Public Salvation,' whereat the world still shrieks and shudders.

If we call that Revolutionary Tribunal a Sword, which Sansculottism has provided for itself, then let us call the 'Law of the Maximum,' a Provender-scrip, or Haversack, wherein better or worse some ration of bread may be found. It is true, Political Economy, Girondin free-trade, and all law of supply and demand, are hereby hurled topsyturvy: but what help? Patriotism must live; the 'cupidity of farmers' seems to have no bowels. Wherefore this Law of the Maximum, fixing the highest price of grains, is, with infinite effort, got passed; and shall gradually extend itself into a Maximum for all manner of comestibles and commodities: with such scrambling and topsyturvying as may be fancied! For now, if, for example, the farmer will not sell? The farmer shall be forced to sell. An accurate Account of what grain he has shall be delivered in to the Constituted Authorities: let him see that he say not too much; for in that case, his rents, taxes and contributions will rise proportionally: let him see that he say not too little; for, on or before a set day, we shall suppose in April, less than one-third of this declared quantity, must remain in his barns, more than two-thirds of it must have been thrashed and sold. One can denounce him, and raise penalties.

By such inextricable overturning of all Commercial relation will Sansculottism keep life in; since not otherwise. On the whole, as Camille Desmoulins says once, "while the Sansculottes fight, the Monsieurs must pay." So there come Impots Progressifs, Ascending Taxes; which consume, with fast-increasing voracity, and 'superfluous-revenue' of men: beyond fifty-pounds a-year you are not exempt; rising into the hundreds you bleed freely; into the thousands and tens of thousands, you bleed gushing. Also there come Requisitions; there comes 'Forced-Loan of a Milliard,' some Fifty-Millions Sterling; which of course they that have must lend. Unexampled enough: it has grown to be no country for the Rich, this; but a country for the Poor! And then if one fly, what steads it? Dead in Law; nay kept alive fifty years yet, for their accursed behoof! In this manner, therefore, it goes; topsyturvying, ca-ira-ing; – and withal there is endless sale of Emigrant National-Property, there is Cambon with endless cornucopia of Assignats. The Trade and Finance of Sansculottism; and how, with Maximum and Bakers'-queues, with Cupidity, Hunger, Denunciation and Paper-money, it led its galvanic-life, and began and ended, – remains the most interesting of all Chapters in Political Economy: still to be written.

All which things are they not clean against Formula? O Girondin Friends, it is not a Republic of the Virtues we are getting; but only a Republic of the Strengths, virtuous and other!

EXTINCT.

It seems doubtful whether any terrestrial Convention had ever met in such circumstances as this National one now does. Tocsin is pealing; Barriers shut; all Paris is on the gaze, or under arms. As many as a Hundred Thousand under arms they count: National Force; and the Armed Volunteers, who should have flown to the Frontiers and La Vendee; but would not, treason being unpunished; and only flew hither and thither! So many, steady under arms, environ the National Tuileries and Garden. There are horse, foot, artillery, sappers with beards: the artillery one can see with their camp-furnaces in this National Garden, heating bullets red, and their match is lighted. Henriot in plumes rides, amid a plumed Staff: all posts and issues are safe; reserves lie out, as far as the Wood of Boulogne; the choicest Patriots nearest the scene. One other circumstance we will note: that a careful Municipality, liberal of camp-furnaces, has not forgotten provision-carts. No member of the Sovereign need now go home to dinner; but can keep rank, – plentiful victual circulating unsought. Does not this People understand Insurrection? Ye, not uninventive, Gualches! –

Therefore let a National Representation, 'mandatories of the Sovereign,' take thought of it. Expulsion of your Twenty-two, and your Commission of Twelve: we stand here till it be done! Deputation after Deputation, in ever stronger language, comes with that message. Barrere proposes a middle course: – Will not perhaps the inculpated Deputies consent to withdraw voluntarily; to make a generous demission, and self-sacrifice for the sake of one's country? Isnard, repentant of that search on which river-bank Paris stood, declares himself ready to demit. Ready also is Te-Deum Fauchet; old Dusaulx of the Bastille, 'vieux radoteur, old dotard,' as Marat calls him, is still readier. On the contrary, Lanjuinais the Breton declares that there is one man who never will demit voluntarily; but will protest to the uttermost, while a voice is left him. And he accordingly goes on protesting; amid rage and clangor; Legendre crying at last: "Lanjuinais, come down from the Tribune, or I will fling thee down, ou je te jette en bas!" For matters are come to extremity. Nay they do clutch hold of Lanjuinais, certain zealous Mountain-men; but cannot fling him down, for he 'cramps himself on the railing;' and 'his clothes get torn.' Brave Senator, worthy of pity! Neither will Barbaroux demit; he "has sworn to die at his post, and will keep that oath." Whereupon the Galleries all rise with explosion; brandishing weapons, some of them;

and rush out saying: "Allons, then; we must save our country!"
Such a Session is this of Sunday the second of June.

Churches fill, over Christian Europe, and then empty
themselves; but this Convention empties not, the while:
a day of shrieking contention, of agony, humiliation and
tearing of coatskirts; illa suprema dies! Round stand Henriot
and his Hundred Thousand, copiously refreshed from tray
and basket: nay he is 'distributing five francs a-piece;' we
Girondins saw it with our eyes; five francs to keep them in
heart! And distraction of armed riot encumbers our borders,
jangles at our Bar; we are prisoners in our own Hall: Bishop
Gregoire could not get out for a besoin actuel without
four gendarmes to wait on him! What is the character of
a National Representative become? And now the sunlight
falls yellower on western windows, and the chimney-tops are
flinging longer shadows; the refreshed Hundred Thousand,
nor their shadows, stir not! What to resolve on? Motion rises,
superfluous one would think, That the Convention go forth
in a body; ascertain with its own eyes whether it is free or
not. Lo, therefore, from the Eastern Gate of the Tuileries, a
distressed Convention issuing; handsome Herault Sechelles
at their head; he with hat on, in sign of public calamity,
the rest bareheaded, – towards the Gate of the Carrousel;
wondrous to see: towards Henriot and his plumed staff. "In
the name of the National Convention, make way!" Not an
inch of the way does Henriot make: "I receive no orders,
till the Sovereign, yours and mine, has been obeyed." The
Convention presses on; Henriot prances back, with his staff,
some fifteen paces, "To arms! Cannoneers to your guns!" –
flashes out his puissant sword, as the Staff all do, and the
Hussars all do. Cannoneers brandish the lit match; Infantry

present arms, – alas, in the level way, as if for firing! Hatted Herault leads his distressed flock, through their pinfold of a Tuileries again; across the Garden, to the Gate on the opposite side. Here is Feuillans Terrace, alas, there is our old Salle de Manege; but neither at this Gate of the Pont Tournant is there egress. Try the other; and the other: no egress! We wander disconsolate through armed ranks; who indeed salute with Live the Republic, but also with Die the Gironde. Other such sight, in the year One of Liberty, the westering sun never saw.

And now behold Marat meets us; for he lagged in this Suppliant Procession of ours: he has got some hundred elect Patriots at his heels: he orders us in the Sovereign's name to return to our place, and do as we are bidden and bound. The Convention returns. "Does not the Convention," says Couthon with a singular power of face, "see that it is free?" – none but friends round it? The Convention, overflowing with friends and armed Sectioners, proceeds to vote as bidden. Many will not vote, but remain silent; some one or two protest, in words: the Mountain has a clear unanimity. Commission of Twelve, and the denounced Twenty-two, to whom we add Ex-Ministers Claviere and Lebrun: these, with some slight extempore alterations (this or that orator proposing, but Marat disposing), are voted to be under 'Arrestment in their own houses.' Brissot, Buzot, Vergniaud, Guadet, Louvet, Gensonne, Barbaroux, Lasource, Lanjuinais, Rabaut, – Thirty-two, by the tale; all that we have known as Girondins, and more than we have known. They, 'under the safeguard of the French People;' by and by, under the safeguard of two Gendarmes each, shall dwell peaceably in their own houses; as Non-Senators; till further order.

Herewith ends Seance of Sunday the second of June 1793.

At ten o'clock, under mild stars, the Hundred Thousand, their work well finished, turn homewards. This same day, Central Insurrection Committee has arrested Madame Roland; imprisoned her in the Abbaye. Roland has fled, no one knows whither.

Thus fell the Girondins, by Insurrection; and became extinct as a Party: not without a sigh from most Historians. The men were men of parts, of Philosophic culture, decent behaviour; not condemnable in that they were Pedants and had not better parts; not condemnable, but most unfortunate. They wanted a Republic of the Virtues, wherein themselves should be head; and they could only get a Republic of the Strengths, wherein others than they were head.

For the rest, Barrere shall make Report of it. The night concludes with a 'civic promenade by torchlight:' surely the true reign of Fraternity is now not far?

CHARLOTTE CORDAY.

In the leafy months of June and July, several French Departments germinate a set of rebellious paper-leaves, named Proclamations, Resolutions, Journals, or Diurnals 'of the Union for Resistance to Oppression.' In particular, the Town of Caen, in Calvados, sees its paper-leaf of Bulletin de Caen suddenly bud, suddenly establish itself as Newspaper there; under the Editorship of Girondin National Representatives!

Amid which dim ferment of Caen and the World, History specially notices one thing: in the lobby of the Mansion de l'Intendance, where busy Deputies are coming and going, a young Lady with an aged valet, taking grave graceful leave of Deputy Barbaroux. She is of stately Norman figure; in her twenty-fifth year; of beautiful still countenance: her name is Charlotte Corday, heretofore styled d'Armans, while Nobility still was. Barbaroux has given her a Note to Deputy Duperret, – him who once drew his sword in the effervescence. Apparently she will to Paris on some errand? 'She was a Republican before the Revolution, and never wanted energy.' A completeness, a decision is in this fair female Figure: 'by energy she means the spirit that will prompt one to sacrifice himself for his country.' What if she, this fair young Charlotte, had emerged from her secluded stillness, suddenly like a Star; cruel-lovely, with half-angelic, half-demonic splendour; to gleam for a moment, and in a moment be extinguished: to be held in memory, so bright complete was she, through long centuries! – Quitting Cimmerian Coalitions without, and the dim-simmering Twenty-five millions within, History will look fixedly at this one fair Apparition of a Charlotte Corday; will note whither Charlotte moves, how the little Life burns forth so radiant, then vanishes swallowed of the Night.

With Barbaroux's Note of Introduction, and slight stock of luggage, we see Charlotte, on Tuesday the ninth of July, seated in the Caen Diligence, with a place for Paris. None takes farewell of her, wishes her Good-journey: her Father will find a line left, signifying that she is gone to England, that he must pardon her and forget her. The drowsy Diligence lumbers along; amid drowsy talk of Politics, and praise of the Mountain; in which she mingles not; all night, all day, and again all night. On Thursday, not long before none, we are at the Bridge of Neuilly; here is Paris with her thousand black domes, – the goal and purpose of thy journey! Arrived at the Inn de la Providence in the Rue des Vieux Augustins, Charlotte demands a room; hastens to bed; sleeps all afternoon and night, till the morrow morning.

On the morrow morning, she delivers her Note to Duperret. It relates to certain Family Papers which are in the Minister of the Interior's hand; which a Nun at Caen, an old Convent-friend of Charlotte's, has need of; which Duperret shall assist her in getting: this then was Charlotte's errand to Paris? She has finished this, in the course of Friday; – yet says nothing of returning. She has seen and silently investigated several things. The Convention, in bodily reality, she has seen; what the Mountain is like. The living physiognomy of Marat she could not see; he is sick at present, and confined to home.

About eight on the Saturday morning, she purchases a large sheath-knife in the Palais Royal; then straightway, in the Place des Victoires, takes a hackney-coach: "To the Rue de l'Ecole de Medecine, No. 44." It is the residence of the Citoyen Marat! – The Citoyen Marat is ill, and cannot be seen; which seems to disappoint her much. Her business is with Marat, then? Hapless beautiful Charlotte; hapless squalid Marat! From Caen in the utmost West, from Neuchatel in the utmost East, they two are drawing nigh each other; they two have, very strangely, business together. – Charlotte, returning to her Inn, despatches a short Note to Marat; signifying that she is from Caen, the seat of rebellion; that she desires earnestly to see him, and 'will put it in his power to do France a great service.' No answer. Charlotte writes another Note, still more pressing; sets out with it by coach, about seven in the evening, herself. Tired day-labourers have again finished their Week; huge Paris is circling and simmering, manifold, according to its vague wont: this one fair Figure has decision in it; drives straight, – towards a purpose.

It is yellow July evening, we say, the thirteenth of the month; eve of the Bastille day, – when 'M. Marat,' four years ago, in the crowd of the Pont Neuf, shrewdly required of that Besenval Hussar-party, which had such friendly dispositions, "to dismount, and give up their arms, then;" and became notable among Patriot men! Four years: what a road he has travelled; – and sits now, about half-past seven of the clock, stewing in slipper-bath; sore afflicted; ill of Revolution Fever, – of what other malady this History had rather not name. Excessively sick and worn, poor man: with precisely elevenpence-halfpenny of ready money, in paper; with slipper-bath; strong three-footed stool for writing on, the while; and a squalid – Washerwoman, one may call her: that is his civic establishment in Medical-School Street; thither and not elsewhither has his road led him. Not to the reign of Brotherhood and Perfect Felicity; yet surely on the way towards that? – Hark, a rap again! A musical woman's-voice, refusing to be rejected: it is the Citoyenne who would do France a service. Marat, recognising from within, cries, Admit her. Charlotte Corday is admitted.

Citoyen Marat, I am from Caen the seat of rebellion, and wished to speak with you. – Be seated, mon enfant. Now what are the Traitors doing at Caen? What Deputies are at Caen? – Charlotte names some Deputies. "Their heads shall fall within a fortnight," croaks the eager People's-Friend, clutching his tablets to write: Barbaroux, Petion, writes he with bare shrunk arm, turning aside in the bath: Petion, and Louvet, and – Charlotte has drawn her knife from the sheath; plunges it, with one sure stroke, into the writer's heart. "A moi, chere amie, Help, dear!" No more could the Death-choked say or shriek. The helpful Washerwoman running in, there is no Friend of the People, or Friend of the Washerwoman, left; but his life with a groan gushes out, indignant, to the shades below.

O NATURE.

But looking more specially into Paris City, what is this that History, on the 10th of August, Year One of Liberty, 'by old-style, year 1793,' discerns there? Praised be the Heavens, a new Feast of Pikes!

For Chaumette's 'Deputation every day' has worked out its result: a Constitution. It was one of the rapidest Constitutions ever put together; made, some say in eight days, by Herault Sechelles and others: probably a workmanlike, roadworthy Constitution enough; – on which point, however, we are, for some reasons, little called to form a judgment. Workmanlike or not, the Forty-four Thousand Communes of France, by overwhelming majorities, did hasten to accept it; glad of any Constitution whatsoever. Nay Departmental Deputies have come, the venerablest Republicans of each Department, with solemn message of Acceptance; and now what remains but that our new Final Constitution be proclaimed, and sworn to, in Feast of Pikes? The Departmental Deputies, we say, are come some time ago; – Chaumette very anxious about them, lest Girondin Monsieurs, Agio-jobbers, or were it even Filles de joie of a Girondin temper, corrupt their morals. Tenth of

August, immortal Anniversary, greater almost than Bastille July, is the Day.

Painter David has not been idle. Thanks to David and the French genius, there steps forth into the sunlight, this day, a Scenic Phantasmagory unexampled: – whereof History, so occupied with Real-Phantasmagories, will say but little.

For one thing, History can notice with satisfaction, on the ruins of the Bastille, a Statue of Nature; gigantic, spouting water from her two mammelles. Not a Dream this; but a Fact, palpable visible. There she spouts, great Nature; dim, before daybreak. But as the coming Sun ruddies the East, come countless Multitudes, regulated and unregulated; come Departmental Deputies, come Mother Society and Daughters; comes National Convention, led on by handsome Herault; soft wind-music breathing note of expectation. Lo, as great Sol scatters his first fire-handful, tipping the hills and chimney-heads with gold, Herault is at great Nature's feet (she is Plaster of Paris merely); Herault lifts, in an iron saucer, water spouted from the sacred breasts; drinks of it, with an eloquent Pagan Prayer, beginning, "O Nature!" and all the Departmental Deputies drink, each with what best suitable ejaculation or prophetic-utterance is in him; – amid breathings, which become blasts, of wind-music; and the roar of artillery and human throats: finishing well the first act of this solemnity.

And now mark, in the Place de la Revolution, what other August Statue may this be; veiled in canvas, – which swiftly we shear off by pulley and cord? The Statue of Liberty! She too is of plaster, hoping to become of metal; stands where a Tyrant Louis Quinze once stood. 'Three thousand birds' are

let loose, into the whole world, with labels round their neck,
We are free; imitate us. Holocaust of Royalist and ci-devant
trumpery, such as one could still gather, is burnt; pontifical
eloquence must be uttered, by handsome Herault, and Pagan
orisons offered up.

And then forward across the River; where is new
enormous Statuary; enormous plaster Mountain; Hercules-
Peuple, with uplifted all-conquering club; 'many-headed
Dragon of Girondin Federalism rising from fetid marsh;'
– needing new eloquence from Herault. To say nothing of
Champ-de-Mars, and Fatherland's Altar there; with urn of
slain Defenders, Carpenter's-level of the Law; and such
exploding, gesticulating and perorating, that Herault's lips
must be growing white, and his tongue cleaving to the roof
of his mouth.

Towards six-o'clock let the wearied President, let Paris
Patriotism generally sit down to what repast, and social
repasts, can be had; and with flowing tankard or light-
mantling glass, usher in this New and Newest Era. In fact, is
not Romme's New Calendar getting ready? On all housetops
flicker little tricolor Flags, their flagstaff a Pike and Liberty-
Cap. On all house-walls, for no Patriot, not suspect, will be
behind another, there stand printed these words: Republic
one and indivisible, Liberty, Equality, Fraternity, or Death.

As to the New Calendar, we may say here rather than
elsewhere that speculative men have long been struck with
the inequalities and incongruities of the Old Calendar; that a
New one has long been as good as determined on. Marechal
the Atheist, almost ten years ago, proposed a New Calendar,
free at least from superstition: this the Paris Municipality
would now adopt, in defect of a better; at all events, let us

have either this of Marechal's or a better, – the New Era being come. Petitions, more than once, have been sent to that effect; and indeed, for a year past, all Public Bodies, Journalists, and Patriots in general, have dated First Year of the Republic. It is a subject not without difficulties. But the Convention has taken it up; and Romme, as we say, has been meditating it; not Marechal's New Calendar, but a better New one of Romme's and our own. Romme, aided by a Monge, a Lagrange and others, furnishes mathematics; Fabre d'Eglantine furnishes poetic nomenclature: and so, on the 5th of October 1793, after trouble enough, they bring forth this New Republican Calendar of theirs, in a complete state; and by Law, get it put in action.

Four equal Seasons, Twelve equal Months of thirty days each: this makes three hundred and sixty days; and five odd days remain to be disposed of. The five odd days we will make Festivals, and name the five Sansculottides, or Days without Breeches. Festival of Genius; Festival of Labour; of Actions; of Rewards; of Opinion: these are the five Sansculottides. Whereby the great Circle, or Year, is made complete: solely every fourth year, whilom called Leap-year, we introduce a sixth Sansculottide; and name it Festival of the Revolution. Now as to the day of commencement, which offers difficulties, is it not one of the luckiest coincidences that the Republic herself commenced on the 21st of September; close on the Vernal Equinox? Vernal Equinox, at midnight for the meridian of Paris, in the year whilom Christian 1792, from that moment shall the New Era reckon itself to begin. Vendemiaire, Brumaire, Frimaire; or as one might say, in mixed English, Vintagearious, Fogarious, Frostarious: these are our three Autumn months. Nivose, Pluviose, Ventose, or say Snowous, Rainous, Windous, make our Winter season. Germinal, Floreal, Prairial, or Buddal, Floweral, Meadowal, are our Spring season. Messidor, Thermidor, Fructidor, that is to say (dor being Greek for gift) Reapidor, Heatidor, Fruitidor, are Republican Summer. These Twelve, in a singular manner, divide the Republican Year. Then as to minuter subdivisions, let us venture at once on a bold stroke: adopt your decimal subdivision; and instead of world-old Week, or Se'ennight, make it a Tennight or Decade; – not without results. There are three Decades, then, in each of the months; which is very regular; and the Decadi, or Tenth-day, shall always be 'the Day of Rest.' And the Christian Sabbath, in that case? Shall shift for itself!

This, in brief, in this New Calendar of Romme and the Convention; calculated for the meridian of Paris, and Gospel of Jean-Jacques: not one of the least afflicting occurrences for the actual British reader of French History; – confusing the soul with Messidors, Meadowals; till at last, in self-defence, one is forced to construct some ground-scheme, or rule of Commutation from New-style to Old-style, and have it lying by him.

Thus with new Feast of Pikes, and New Era or New Calendar, did France accept her New Constitution: the most Democratic Constitution ever committed to paper. How it will work in practice? Patriot Deputations from time to time solicit fruition of it; that it be set a-going. Always, however, this seems questionable; for the moment, unsuitable. Till, in some weeks, Salut Public, through the organ of Saint-Just, makes report, that, in the present alarming circumstances, the state of France is Revolutionary; that her 'Government must be Revolutionary till the Peace!' Solely as Paper, then, and as a Hope, must this poor New Constitution exist; – in which shape we may conceive it lying; even now, with an infinity of other things, in that Limbo near the Moon. Further than paper it never got, nor ever will get.

RISEN AGAINST TYRANTS.

Against all which incalculable impediments, horrors and disasters, what can a Jacobin Convention oppose? The uncalculating Spirit of Jacobinism, and Sansculottic sans-formulistic Frenzy! Our Enemies press in on us, says Danton, but they shall not conquer us, "we will burn France to ashes rather, nous brulerons la France."

Committees, of Surete or Salut, have raised themselves 'a la hauteur, to the height of circumstances.' Let all mortals raise themselves a la hauteur. Let the Forty-four thousand Sections and their Revolutionary Committees stir every fibre of the Republic; and every Frenchman feel that he is to do or die. They are the life-circulation of Jacobinism, these Sections and Committees: Danton, through the organ of Barrere and Salut Public, gets decreed, That there be in Paris, by law, two meetings of Section weekly; also, that the Poorer Citizen be paid for attending, and have his day's-wages of Forty Sous. This is the celebrated 'Law of the Forty Sous;' fiercely stimulant to Sansculottism, to the life-circulation of Jacobinism.

On the twenty-third of August, Committee of Public Sal-vation, as usual through Barrere, had promulgated, in words not unworthy of remembering, their Report, which is soon made into a Law, of Levy in Mass. 'All France, and whatsoever it contains of men or resources, is put under requisition,' says Barrere; really in Tyrtaean words, the best we know of his. 'The Republic is one vast besieged city.' Two hundred and fifty Forges shall, in these days, be set up in the Luxembourg Garden, and round the outer wall of the Tuileries; to make gun-barrels; in sight of Earth and Heaven! From all hamlets, towards their Departmental Town; from all their Departmental Towns, towards the appointed Camp and seat of war, the Sons of Freedom shall march; their banner is to bear: 'Le Peuple Francais debout contres les Tyrans, The French People risen against Tyrants.' 'The young men shall go to the battle; it is their task to conquer: the married men shall forge arms, transport baggage and artillery; provide subsistence: the women shall work at soldiers' clothes, make tents; serve in the hospitals. The children shall scrape old-linen into surgeon's-lint: the aged men shall have themselves carried into public places; and there, by their words, excite the courage of the young; preach hatred to Kings and unity to the Republic.' Tyrtaean words, which tingle through all French hearts.

In this humour, then, since no other serves, will France rush against its enemies. Headlong, reckoning no cost or consequence; heeding no law or rule but that supreme law, Salvation of the People! The weapons are all the iron that is in France; the strength is that of all the men, women and children that are in France. There, in their two hundred and fifty shed-smithies, in Garden of Luxembourg or Tuileries, let them forge gun-barrels, in sight of Heaven and Earth.

Nor with heroic daring against the Foreign foe, can black vengeance against the Domestic be wanting. Life-circulation of the Revolutionary Committees being quickened by that Law of the Forty Sous, Deputy Merlin, not the Thionviller, whom we saw ride out of Mentz, but Merlin of Douai, named subsequently Merlin Suspect, – comes, about a week after, with his world-famous Law of the Suspect: ordering all Sections, by their Committees, instantly to arrest all Persons Suspect; and explaining withal who the Arrestable and Suspect specially are. "Are Suspect," says he, "all who by their actions, by their connexions, speakings, writings have" – in short become Suspect. Nay Chaumette, illuminating the matter still further, in his Municipal Placards and Proclamations, will bring it about that you may almost recognise a Suspect on the streets, and clutch him there, – off to Committee, and Prison. Watch well your words, watch well your looks: if Suspect of nothing else, you may grow, as came to be a saying, 'Suspect of being Suspect!' For are we not in a State of Revolution?

No frightfuller Law ever ruled in a Nation of men. All Prisons and Houses of Arrest in French land are getting crowded to the ridge-tile: Forty-four thousand Committees, like as many companies of reapers or gleaners, gleaning France, are gathering their harvest, and storing it in these Houses. Harvest of Aristocrat tares! Nay, lest the Forty-four thousand, each on its own harvest-field, prove insufficient, we are to have an ambulant 'Revolutionary Army:' six thousand strong, under right captains, this shall perambulate the country at large, and strike in wherever it finds such harvest-work slack. So have Municipality and Mother Society petitioned; so has Convention decreed. Let Aristocrats, Federalists, Monsieurs vanish, and all men tremble: 'The Soil of Liberty shall be purged,' – with a vengeance!

Neither hitherto has the Revolutionary Tribunal been keeping holyday. Blanchelande, for losing Saint-Domingo;

'Conspirators of Orleans,' for 'assassinating,' for assaulting the sacred Deputy Leonard-Bourdon: these with many Nameless, to whom life was sweet, have died. Daily the great Guillotine has its due. Like a black Spectre, daily at eventide, glides the Death-tumbril through the variegated throng of things. The variegated street shudders at it, for the moment; next moment forgets it: The Aristocrats! They were guilty against the Republic; their death, were it only that their goods are confiscated, will be useful to the Republic; Vive la Republique!

RUSHING DOWN.

We are now, therefore, got to that black precipitous Abyss; whither all things have long been tending; where, having now arrived on the giddy verge, they hurl down, in confused ruin; headlong, pellmell, down, down; – till Sansculottism have consummated itself; and in this wondrous French Revolution, as in a Doomsday, a World have been rapidly, if not born again, yet destroyed and engulphed. Terror has long been terrible: but to the actors themselves it has now become manifest that their appointed course is one of Terror; and they say, Be it so. "Que la Terreur soit a l'ordre du jour."

So many centuries, say only from Hugh Capet downwards, had been adding together, century transmitting it with increase to century, the sum of Wickedness, of Falsehood, Oppression of man by man. Kings were sinners, and Priests were, and People. Open-Scoundrels rode triumphant, bediademed, becoronetted, bemitred; or the still fataller species of Secret-Scoundrels, in their fair-sounding formulas, speciosities, respectabilities, hollow within: the race of

163

Quacks was grown many as the sands of the sea. Till at length such a sum of Quackery had accumulated itself as, in brief, the Earth and the Heavens were weary of. Slow seemed the Day of Settlement: coming on, all imperceptible, across the bluster and fanfaronade of Courtierisms, Conquering-Heroisms, Most-Christian Grand Monarque-isms. Well-beloved Pompadourisms: yet behold it was always coming; behold it has come, suddenly, unlooked for by any man! The harvest of long centuries was ripening and whitening so rapidly of late; and now it is grown white, and is reaped rapidly, as it were, in one day. Reaped, in this Reign of Terror; and carried home, to Hades and the Pit! – Unhappy Sons of Adam: it is ever so; and never do they know it, nor will they know it. With cheerfully smoothed countenances, day after day, and generation after generation, they, calling cheerfully to one another, "Well-speed-ye," are at work, sowing the wind. And yet, as God lives, they shall reap the whirlwind: no other thing, we say, is possible, – since God is a Truth and His World is a Truth.

History, however, in dealing with this Reign of Terror, has had her own difficulties. While the Phenomenon continued in its primary state, as mere 'Horrors of the French Revolution,' there was abundance to be said and shrieked. With and also without profit. Heaven knows there were terrors and horrors enough: yet that was not all the Phenomenon; nay, more properly, that was not the Phenomenon at all, but rather was the shadow of it, the negative part of it. And now, in a new stage of the business, when History, ceasing to shriek, would try rather to include under her old Forms of speech or speculation this new amazing Thing; that so some accredited scientific Law of Nature might suffice for the unexpected Product of Nature, and History might get to speak of it articulately, and draw inferences and profit from it; in this new stage, History, we must say, babbles and flounders perhaps in a still painfuller manner. Take, for example, the latest Form of speech we have seen propounded on the subject as adequate to it, almost in these months, by our worthy M. Roux, in his Histoire Parlementaire. The latest and the strangest: that the French Revolution was a dead-lift effort, after eighteen hundred years of preparation, to realise – the Christian Religion! Unity, Indivisibility, Brotherhood or Death did indeed stand printed on all Houses of the Living; also, on Cemeteries, or Houses of the Dead, stood printed, by order of Procureur Chaumette, Here is eternal Sleep: but a Christian Religion realised by the Guillotine and Death-Eternal, 'is suspect to me,' as Robespierre was wont to say, 'm'est suspecte.'

Alas, no, M. Roux! A Gospel of Brotherhood, not according to any of the Four old Evangelists, and calling on men to repent, and amend each his own wicked existence, that they might be saved; but a Gospel rather, as we often hint, according to a new Fifth Evangelist Jean-Jacques, calling on men to amend each the whole world's wicked existence, and be saved by making the Constitution. A thing different and distant toto coelo, as they say: the whole breadth of the sky, and further if possible! – It is thus, however, that History, and indeed all human Speech and Reason does yet, what Father Adam began life by doing: strive to name the new Things it sees of Nature's producing, – often helplessly enough.

But what if History were to admit, for once, that all the Names and Theorems yet known to her fall short? That this grand Product of Nature was even grand, and new, in that it came not to range itself under old recorded Laws-of-Nature at all; but to disclose new ones? In that case, History renouncing the pretention to name it at present, will look honestly at it, and name what she can of it! Any approximation to the right Name has value: were the right name itself once here, the Thing is known thenceforth; the Thing is then ours, and can be dealt with.

Now surely not realization, of Christianity, or of aught earthly, do we discern in this Reign of Terror, in this French Revolution of which it is the consummating. Destruction rather we discern – of all that was destructible. It is as if Twenty-five millions, risen at length into the Pythian mood, had stood up simultaneously to say, with a sound which goes through far lands and times, that this Untruth of an Existence had become insupportable. O ye Hypocrisies and Speciosities, Royal mantles, Cardinal plushcloaks, ye Credos, Formulas, Respectabilities, fair-painted Sepulchres full of dead men's bones, – behold, ye appear to us to be altogether a Lie. Yet our Life is not a Lie; yet our Hunger and Misery is not a Lie! Behold we lift up, one and all, our Twenty-five million right-hands; and take the Heavens, and the Earth and also the Pit of Tophet to witness, that either ye shall be abolished, or else we shall be abolished!

No inconsiderable Oath, truly; forming, as has been often said, the most remarkable transaction in these last thousand years. Wherefrom likewise there follow, and will follow, results. The fulfilment of this Oath; that is to say, the black desperate battle of Men against their whole Condition and Environment, – a battle, alas, withal, against the Sin and Darkness that was in themselves as in others: this is the

Reign of Terror. Transcendental despair was the purport of it, though not consciously so. False hopes, of Fraternity, Political Millennium, and what not, we have always seen: but the unseen heart of the whole, the transcendental despair, was not false; neither has it been of no effect. Despair, pushed far enough, completes the circle, so to speak; and becomes a kind of genuine productive hope again.

Doctrine of Fraternity, out of old Catholicism, does, it is true, very strangely in the vehicle of a Jean-Jacques Evangel, suddenly plump down out of its cloud-firmament; and from a theorem determine to make itself a practice. But just so do all creeds, intentions, customs, knowledges, thoughts and things, which the French have, suddenly plump down; Catholicism, Classicism, Sentimentalism, Cannibalism: all isms that make up Man in France, are rushing and roaring in that gulf; and the theorem has become a practice, and whatsoever cannot swim sinks. Not Evangelist Jean-Jacques alone; there is not a Village Schoolmaster but has contributed his quota: do we not 'thou' one another, according to the Free Peoples of Antiquity? The French Patriot, in red phrygian nightcap of Liberty, christens his poor little red infant Cato, – Censor, or else of Utica. Gracchus has become Baboeuf and edits Newspapers; Mutius Scaevola, Cordwainer of that ilk, presides in the Section Mutius-Scaevola: and in brief, there is a world wholly jumbling itself, to try what will swim!

Wherefore we will, at all events, call this Reign of Terror a very strange one. Dominant Sansculottism makes, as it were, free arena; one of the strangest temporary states Humanity was ever seen in. A nation of men, full of wants and void of habits! The old habits are gone to wreck because they were old: men, driven forward by Necessity and fierce Pythian

Madness, have, on the spur of the instant, to devise for the want the way of satisfying it. The wonted tumbles down; by imitation, by invention, the Unwonted hastily builds itself up. What the French National head has in it comes out: if not a great result, surely one of the strangest.

Neither shall the reader fancy that it was all blank, this Reign of Terror: far from it. How many hammermen and squaremen, bakers and brewers, washers and wringers, over this France, must ply their old daily work, let the Government be one of Terror or one of Joy! In this Paris there are Twenty-three Theatres nightly; some count as many as Sixty Places of Dancing. The Playwright manufactures: pieces of a strictly Republican character. Ever fresh Novelgarbage, as of old, fodders the Circulating Libraries. The 'Cesspool of Agio,' now in the time of Paper Money, works with a vivacity unexampled, unimagined; exhales from itself 'sudden fortunes,' like Alladin-Palaces: really a kind of miraculous Fata-Morganas, since you can live in them, for a time. Terror is as a sable ground, on which the most variegated of scenes paints itself. In startling transitions, in colours all intensated, the sublime, the ludicrous, the horrible succeed one another; or rather, in crowding tumult, accompany one another.

Here, accordingly, if anywhere, the 'hundred tongues,' which the old Poets often clamour for, were of supreme service! In defect of any such organ on our part, let the Reader stir up his own imaginative organ: let us snatch for him this or the other significant glimpse of things, in the fittest sequence we can.

THE GODS ARE ATHIRST.

What then is this Thing, called La Revolution, which, like an Angel of Death, hangs over France, noyading, fusillading, fighting, gun-boring, tanning human skins? La Revolution is but so many Alphabetic Letters; a thing nowhere to be laid hands on, to be clapt under lock and key: where is it? what is it? It is the Madness that dwells in the hearts of men. In this man it is, and in that man; as a rage or as a terror, it is in all men. Invisible, impalpable; and yet no black Azrael, with wings spread over half a continent, with sword sweeping from sea to sea, could be a truer Reality.

To explain, what is called explaining, the march of this Revolutionary Government, be no task of ours. Men cannot explain it. A paralytic Couthon, asking in the Jacobins, 'what hast thou done to be hanged if the Counter-Revolution should arrive;' a sombre Saint-Just, not yet six-and-twenty, declaring that 'for Revolutionists there is no rest but in the tomb;' a seagreen Robespierre converted into vinegar and gall; much more an Amar and Vadier, a Collot and Billaud: to inquire what thoughts, predetermination or prevision, might be in the head of these men! Record of their thought remains not; Death and Darkness have swept it out utterly. Nay if we even had their thought, all they could have articulately spoken to us, how insignificant a fraction were that of the Thing which realised itself, which decreed itself, on signal given by them! As has been said more than once, this Revolutionary Government is not a self-conscious but a blind fatal one. Each man, enveloped in his ambient-atmosphere of revolutionary fanatic Madness, rushes on, impelled and impelling; and has become a blind brute Force;

no rest for him but in the grave! Darkness and the mystery of horrid cruelty cover it for us, in History; as they did in Nature. The chaotic Thunder-cloud, with its pitchy black, and its tumult of dazzling jagged fire, in a world all electric: thou wilt not undertake to shew how that comported itself, – what the secrets of its dark womb were; from what sources, with what specialities, the lightning it held did, in confused brightness of terror, strike forth, destructive and self-destructive, till it ended? Like a Blackness naturally of Erebus, which by will of Providence had for once mounted itself into dominion and the Azure: is not this properly the nature of Sansculottism consummating itself? Of which Erebus Blackness be it enough to discern that this and the other dazzling fire-bolt, dazzling fire-torrent, does by small Volition and great Necessity, verily issue, – in such and such succession; destructive so and so, self-destructive so and so: till it end.

The great heart of Danton is weary of it. Danton is gone to native Arcis, for a little breathing time of peace: Away, black Arachne-webs, thou world of Fury, Terror, and Suspicion; welcome, thou everlasting Mother, with thy spring greenness, thy kind household loves and memories; true art thou, were all else untrue! The great Titan walks silent, by the banks of the murmuring Aube, in young native haunts that knew him when a boy; wonders what the end of these things may be.

But strangest of all, Camille Desmoulins is purged out. Couthon gave as a test in regard to Jacobin purgation the question, 'What hast thou done to be hanged if Counter-Revolution should arrive?' Yet Camille, who could so well answer this question, is purged out! The truth is, Camille, early in December last, began publishing a new Journal, or Series of Pamphlets, entitled the Vieux Cordelier, Old Cordelier. Camille, not afraid at one time to 'embrace Liberty on a heap of dead bodies,' begins to ask now, Whether among so many arresting and punishing Committees there ought not to be a 'Committee of Mercy?' Saint-Just, he observes, is an extremely solemn young Republican, who 'carries his head as if it were a Saint-Sacrement; adorable Hostie, or divine Real-Presence! Sharply enough, this old Cordelier, Danton and he were of the earliest primary Cordeliers, – shoots his glittering war-shafts into your new Cordeliers, your Heberts, Momoros, with their brawling brutalities and despicabilities: say, as the Sun-god (for poor Camille is a Poet) shot into that Python Serpent sprung of mud.

Whereat, as was natural, the Hebertist Python did hiss and writhe amazingly; and threaten 'sacred right of Insurrection;' – and, as we saw, get cast into Prison. Nay, with all the old wit, dexterity, and light graceful poignancy, Camille, translating 'out of Tacitus, from the Reign of Tiberius,' pricks into the Law of the Suspect itself; making it odious! Twice, in the Decade, his wild Leaves issue; full of wit, nay of humour, of harmonious ingenuity and insight, – one of the strangest phenomenon of that dark time; and smite, in their wild-sparkling way, at various monstrosities, Saint-Sacrement heads, and Juggernaut idols, in a rather reckless manner. To the great joy of Josephine Beauharnais, and the other Five Thousand and odd Suspect, who fill the Twelve Houses of Arrest; on whom a ray of hope dawns! Robespierre, at first approbatory, knew not at last what to think; then thought, with his Jacobins, that Camille must be expelled. A man of true Revolutionary spirit, this Camille; but with the unwisest sallies; whom Aristocrats and Moderates have the art to corrupt! Jacobinism is in uttermost crisis and struggle: enmeshed wholly in plots, corruptibilities, neck-gins and baited falltraps of Pitt Ennemi du Genre Humain. Camille's First Number begins with 'O Pitt!' – his last is dated 15 Pluviose Year 2, 3d February 1794; and ends with these words of Montezuma's, 'Les dieux ont soif, The gods are athirst.'

DANTON, NO WEAKNESS.

Danton, meanwhile, has been pressingly sent for from Arcis: he must return instantly, cried Camille, cried Phelippeaux and Friends, who scented danger in the wind. Danger enough! A Danton, a Robespierre, chief-products of a victorious Revolution, are now arrived in immediate front of one another; must ascertain how they will live together, rule together. One conceives easily the deep mutual incompatibility that divided these two: with what terror of feminine hatred the poor seagreen Formula looked at the monstrous colossal Reality, and grew greener to behold him; – the Reality, again, struggling to think no ill of a chief-product of the Revolution; yet feeling at bottom that such chief-product was little other than a chief wind-bag, blown large by Popular air; not a man with the heart of a man, but a poor spasmodic incorruptible pedant, with a logic-formula instead of heart; of Jesuit or Methodist-Parson nature; full of sincere-cant, incorruptibility, of virulence, poltroonery; barren as the east-wind! Two such chief-products are too much for one Revolution.

Friends, trembling at the results of a quarrel on their part, brought them to meet. "It is right," said Danton, swallowing much indignation, "to repress the Royalists: but we should not strike except where it is useful to the Republic; we should not confound the innocent and the guilty." – "And who told you," replied Robespierre with a poisonous look, "that one innocent person had perished?" – "Quoi," said Danton, turning round to Friend Paris self-named Fabricius, Juryman in the Revolutionary Tribunal: "Quoi, not one innocent? What sayest thou of it, Fabricius!" Friends, Westermann, this Paris and others urged him to shew himself, to ascend the Tribune and act. The man Danton was not prone to shew himself; to act, or uproar for his own safety. A man of careless, large, hoping nature; a large nature that could rest: he would sit whole hours, they say, hearing Camille talk, and liked nothing so well. Friends urged him to fly; his Wife urged him: "Whither fly?" answered he: "If freed France cast me out, there are only dungeons for me elsewhere. One carries not his country with him at the sole of his shoe!" The man Danton sat still. Not even the arrestment of Friend Herault, a member of Salut, yet arrested by Salut, can rouse Danton. – On the night of the 30th of March, Juryman Paris came rushing in; haste looking through his eyes: A clerk of the Salut Committee had told him Danton's warrant was made out, he is to be arrested this very night! Entreaties there are and trepidation, of poor Wife, of Paris and Friends: Danton sat silent for a while; then answered, "Ils n'oseraient, They dare not;" and would take no measures. Murmuring "They dare not," he goes to sleep as usual.

And yet, on the morrow morning, strange rumour spreads over Paris City: Danton, Camille, Phelippeaux, Lacroix have been arrested overnight! It is verily so: the corridors of the

Luxembourg were all crowded, Prisoners crowding forth to see this giant of the Revolution among them. "Messieurs," said Danton politely, "I hoped soon to have got you all out of this: but here I am myself; and one sees not where it will end." – Rumour may spread over Paris: the Convention clusters itself into groups; wide-eyed, whispering, "Danton arrested!" Who then is safe? Legendre, mounting the Tribune, utters, at his own peril, a feeble word for him; moving that he be heard at that Bar before indictment; but Robespierre frowns him down: "Did you hear Chabot, or Bazire? Would you have two weights and measures?" Legendre cowers low; Danton, like the others, must take his doom.

Danton's Prison-thoughts were curious to have; but are not given in any quantity: indeed few such remarkable men have been left so obscure to us as this Titan of the Revolution. He was heard to ejaculate: "This time twelvemonth, I was moving the creation of that same Revolutionary Tribunal. I crave pardon for it of God and man. They are all Brothers Cain: Brissot would have had me guillotined as Robespierre now will. I leave the whole business in a frightful welter (gachis epouvantable): not one of them understands anything of government. Robespierre will follow me; I drag down Robespierre. O, it were better to be a poor fisherman than to meddle with governing of men." – Camille's young beautiful Wife, who had made him rich not in money alone, hovers round the Luxembourg, like a disembodied spirit, day and night. Camille's stolen letters to her still exist; stained with the mark of his tears. (Apercus sur Camille Desmoulins in Vieux Cordelier, Paris, 1825, pp. 1-29.) "I carry my head like a Saint-Sacrament?" so Saint-Just was heard to mutter: "Perhaps he will carry his like a Saint-Dennis."

Unhappy Danton, thou still unhappier light Camille, once light Procureur de la Lanterne, ye also have arrived, then, at the Bourne of Creation, where, like Ulysses Polytlas at the limit and utmost Gades of his voyage, gazing into that dim Waste beyond Creation, a man does see the Shade of his Mother, pale, ineffectual; – and days when his Mother nursed and wrapped him are all-too sternly contrasted with this day! Danton, Camille, Herault, Westermann, and the others, very strangely massed up with Bazires, Swindler Chabots, Fabre d'Eglantines, Banker Freys, a most motley Batch, 'Fournee' as such things will be called, stand ranked at the Bar of Tinville. It is the 2d of April 1794. Danton has had but three days to lie in Prison; for the time presses.

What is your name? place of abode? and the like, Fouquier asks; according to formality. "My name is Danton," answers he; "a name tolerably known in the Revolution: my abode will soon be Annihilation (dans le Neant); but I shall live in the Pantheon of History." A man will endeavour to say something forcible, be it by nature or not! Herault mentions epigrammatically that he "sat in this Hall, and was detested of Parlementeers." Camille makes answer, "My age is that of the bon Sansculotte Jesus; an age fatal to Revolutionists." O Camille, Camille! And yet in that Divine Transaction, let us say, there did lie, among other things, the fatallest Reproof ever uttered here below to Worldly Right-honourableness; 'the highest Fact,' so devout Novalis calls it, 'in the Rights of Man.' Camille's real age, it would seem, is thirty-four. Danton is one year older.

Some five months ago, the Trial of the Twenty-two Girondins was the greatest that Fouquier had then done. But here is a still greater to do; a thing which tasks the whole faculty of Fouquier; which makes the very heart of him waver. For it is the voice of Danton that reverberates now from these domes; in passionate words, piercing with their wild sincerity, winged with wrath. Your best Witnesses he shivers into ruin at one stroke. He demands that the Committee-men themselves come as Witnesses, as Accusers; he "will cover them with ignominy." He raises his huge stature, he shakes his huge black head, fire flashes from the eyes of him, – piercing to all Republican hearts: so that the very Galleries, though we filled them by ticket, murmur sympathy; and are like to burst down, and raise the People, and deliver him! He complains loudly that he is classed with Chabots, with swindling Stockjobbers; that his Indictment is a list of platitudes and horrors. "Danton hidden on the Tenth of August?" reverberates he, with the roar of a lion in the toils: "Where are the men that had to press Danton to shew himself, that day? Where are these high-gifted souls of whom he borrowed energy? Let them appear, these Accusers of mine: I have all the clearness of my self-possession when I demand them. I will unmask the three shallow scoundrels," les trois plats coquins, Saint-Just, Couthon, Lebas, "who fawn on Robespierre, and lead him towards his destruction. Let them produce themselves here; I will plunge them into Nothingness, out of which they ought never to have risen." The agitated President agitates his bell; enjoins calmness, in a vehement manner: "What is it to thee how I defend myself?" cries the other: "the right of dooming me is thine always. The voice of a man speaking for his honour and his life may well drown the jingling of thy bell!" Thus Danton, higher and higher; till the lion voice of him 'dies away in his throat:' speech will not utter what is in that man. The Galleries murmur ominously; the first day's Session is over.

O Tinville, President Herman, what will ye do? They have two days more of it, by strictest Revolutionary Law. The Galleries already murmur. If this Danton were to burst your mesh-work! – Very curious indeed to consider. It turns on a hair: and what a Hoitytoity were there, Justice and Culprit changing places; and the whole History of France running changed! For in France there is this Danton only that could still try to govern France. He only, the wild amorphous Titan; – and perhaps that other olive-complexioned individual, the Artillery Officer at Toulon, whom we left pushing his fortune in the South?

On the evening of the second day, matters looking not better but worse and worse, Fouquier and Herman, distraction in their aspect, rush over to Salut Public. What is to be done? Salut Public rapidly concocts a new Decree; whereby if men 'insult Justice,' they may be 'thrown out of the Debates.' For indeed, withal, is there not 'a Plot in the Luxembourg Prison?' Ci-devant General Dillon, and others of the Suspect, plotting with Camille's Wife to distribute assignats; to force the Prisons, overset the Republic? Citizen Laflotte, himself Suspect but desiring enfranchisement, has reported said Plot for us: – a report that may bear fruit! Enough, on the morrow morning, an obedient Convention passes this Decree. Salut rushes off with it to the aid of Tinville, reduced now almost to extremities. And so, Hors des Debats, Out of the Debates, ye insolents! Policemen do your duty! In such manner, with a deadlift effort, Salut, Tinville Herman, Leroi Dix-Aout, and all stanch jurymen setting heart and shoulder to it, the Jury becomes 'sufficiently instructed;' Sentence is passed, is sent by an Official, and torn and trampled on: Death this day. It is the 5th of April, 1794. Camille's poor Wife may cease hovering about this Prison. Nay let her kiss her poor children; and prepare to enter it, and to follow! –

Danton carried a high look in the Death-cart. Not so Camille: it is but one week, and all is so topsy-turvied; angel Wife left weeping; love, riches, Revolutionary fame, left all at the Prison-gate; carnivorous Rabble now howling round. Palpable, and yet incredible; like a madman's dream! Camille struggles and writhes; his shoulders shuffle the loose coat off them, which hangs knotted, the hands tied: "Calm my friend," said Danton; "heed not that vile canaille (laissez la cette vile canaille)." At the foot of the Scaffold, Danton was heard to ejaculate: "O my Wife, my well-beloved, I shall never see thee more then!" – but, interrupting himself: "Danton, no weakness!" He said to Herault-Sechelles stepping forward to embrace him: "Our heads will meet there," in the Headsman's sack. His last words were to Samson the Headsman himself: "Thou wilt shew my head to the people; it is worth shewing."

So passes, like a gigantic mass, of valour, ostentation, fury, affection and wild revolutionary manhood, this Danton, to his unknown home. He was of Arcis-sur-Aube; born of 'good farmer-people' there. He had many sins; but one worst sin he had not, that of Cant. No hollow Formalist, deceptive and self-deceptive, ghastly to the natural sense, was this; but a very Man: with all his dross he was a Man; fiery-real, from the great fire-bosom of Nature herself. He saved France from Brunswick; he walked straight his own wild road, whither it led him. He may live for some generations in the memory of men.

THE FRENCH REVOLUTION

MUMBO-JUMBO.

But on the day they call Decadi, New-Sabbath, 20 Prairial, 8th June by old style, what thing is this going forward, in the Jardin National, whilom Tuileries Garden?

All the world is there, in holydays clothes: foul linen went out with the Hebertists; nay Robespierre, for one, would never once countenance that; but went always elegant and frizzled, not without vanity even, – and had his room hung round with seagreen Portraits and Busts. In holyday clothes, we say, are the innumerable Citoyens and Citoyennes: the weather is of the brightest; cheerful expectation lights all countenances. Juryman Vilate gives breakfast to many a Deputy, in his official Apartment, in the Pavillon ci-devant of Flora; rejoices in the bright-looking multitudes, in the brightness of leafy June, in the auspicious Decadi, or New-Sabbath. This day, if it please Heaven, we are to have, on improved Anti-Chaumette principles: a New Religion.

Catholicism being burned out, and Reason-worship guillotined, was there not need of one? Incorruptible Robespierre, not unlike the Ancients, as Legislator of a free people will now also be Priest and Prophet. He has donned his sky-blue coat, made for the occasion; white silk waistcoat broidered with silver, black silk breeches, white stockings, shoe-buckles of gold. He is President of the Convention; he has made the Convention decree, so they name it, decreter the 'Existence of the Supreme Being,' and likewise 'ce principe consolateur of the Immortality of the Soul.' These consolatory principles, the basis of rational Republican Religion, are getting decreed; and here, on this blessed Decadi, by help of Heaven and Painter David, is to be our first act of worship.

See, accordingly, how after Decree passed, and what has been called 'the scraggiest Prophetic Discourse ever uttered by man,' – Mahomet Robespierre, in sky-blue coat and black breeches, frizzled and powdered to perfection, bearing in his hand a bouquet of flowers and wheat-ears, issues proudly from the Convention Hall; Convention following him, yet, as is remarked, with an interval. Amphitheatre has been raised, or at least Monticule or Elevation; hideous Statues of Atheism, Anarchy and such like, thanks to Heaven and Painter David, strike abhorrence into the heart. Unluckily however, our Monticule is too small. On the top of it not half of us can stand; wherefore there arises indecent shoving, nay treasonous irreverent growling. Peace, thou Bourdon de l'Oise; peace, or it may be worse for thee!

The seagreen Pontiff takes a torch, Painter David handing it; mouths some other froth-rant of vocables, which happily one cannot hear; strides resolutely forward, in sight of expectant France; sets his torch to Atheism and Company, which are but made of pasteboard steeped in turpentine. They burn up rapidly; and, from within, there rises 'by machinery' an incombustible Statue of Wisdom, which, by ill hap, gets besmoked a little; but does stand there visible in as serene attitude as it can.

And then? Why, then, there is other Processioning, scraggy Discoursing, and – this is our Feast of the Etre Supreme; our new Religion, better or worse, is come! – Look at it one moment, O Reader, not two. The Shabbiest page of Human Annals: or is there, that thou wottest of, one shabbier? Mumbo-Jumbo of the African woods to me seems venerable beside this new Deity of Robespierre; for this is a conscious Mumbo-Jumbo, and knows that he is machinery. O seagreen

Prophet, unhappiest of windbags blown nigh to bursting, what distracted Chimera among realities are thou growing to! This then, this common pitch-link for artificial fireworks of turpentine and pasteboard; this is the miraculous Aaron's Rod thou wilt stretch over a hag-ridden hell-ridden France, and bid her plagues cease? Vanish, thou and it! – "Avec ton Etre Supreme," said Billaud, "tu commences m'embeter: With thy Etre Supreme thou beginnest to be a bore to me."

Catherine Theot, on the other hand, 'an ancient serving-maid seventy-nine years of age,' inured to Prophecy and the Bastille from of old, sits, in an upper room in the Rue-de-Contrescarpe, poring over the Book of Revelations, with an eye to Robespierre; finds that this astonishing thrice-potent Maximilien really is the Man spoken of by Prophets, who is to make the Earth young again. With her sit devout old Marchionesses, ci-devant honourable women; among whom Old-Constituent Dom Gerle, with his addle head, cannot be wanting. They sit there, in the Rue-de-Contrescarpe; in mysterious adoration: Mumbo is Mumbo, and Robespierre is his Prophet. A conspicuous man this Robespierre. He has his volunteer Bodyguard of Tappe-durs, let us say Strike-sharps, fierce Patriots with feruled sticks; and Jacobins kissing the hem of his garment. He enjoys the admiration of many, the worship of some; and is well worth the wonder of one and all.

The grand question and hope, however, is: Will not this Feast of the Tuileries Mumbo-Jumbo be a sign perhaps that the Guillotine is to abate? Far enough from that! Precisely on the second day after it, Couthon, one of the 'three shallow scoundrels,' gets himself lifted into the Tribune; produces a bundle of papers. Couthon proposes that, as Plots still abound, the Law of the Suspect shall have extension, and Arrestment new vigour and facility. Further that, as in such case business is like to be heavy, our Revolutionary Tribunal too shall have extension; be divided, say, into Four Tribunals, each with its President, each with its Fouquier or Substitute of Fouquier, all labouring at once, and any remnant of shackle or dilatory formality be struck off: in this way it may perhaps still overtake the work. Such is Couthon's Decree of the Twenty-second Prairial, famed in those times. At hearing of which Decree the very Mountain gasped, awestruck; and one Ruamps ventured to say that if it passed without adjournment and discussion, he, as one Representative, "would blow his brains out." Vain saying! The Incorruptible knit his brows; spoke a prophetic fateful word or two: the Law of Prairial is Law; Ruamps glad to leave his rash brains where they are. Death, then, and always Death! Even so. Fouquier is enlarging his borders; making room for Batches of a Hundred and fifty at once; – getting a Guillotine set up, of improved velocity, and to work under cover, in the apartment close by. So that Salut itself has to intervene, and forbid him: "Wilt thou demoralise the Guillotine," asks Collot, reproachfully, "demoraliser le supplice!"

There is indeed danger of that; were not the Republican faith great, it were already done. See, for example, on the 17th of June, what a Batch, Fifty-four at once! Swart Amiral is here, he of the pistol that missed fire; young Cecile Renault, with her father, family, entire kith and kin; the widow of d'Espremenil; old M. de Sombreuil of the Invalides, with his Son, – poor old Sombreuil, seventy-three years old, his Daughter saved him in September, and it was but for this. Faction of the Stranger, fifty-four of them! In red shirts and smocks, as Assassins and Faction of the Stranger, they flit along there; red baleful Phantasmagory, towards the land of Phantoms.

Meanwhile will not the people of the Place de la Revolution, the inhabitants along the Rue Saint-Honore, as these continual Tumbrils pass, begin to look gloomy? Republicans too have bowels. The Guillotine is shifted, then again shifted; finally set up at the remote extremity of the South-East: Suburbs Saint-Antoine and Saint-Marceau it is to be hoped, if they have bowels, have very tough ones.

TO FINISH THE TERROR.

It is very remarkable, indeed, that since the Etre-Supreme Feast, and the sublime continued harangues on it, which Billaud feared would become a bore to him, Robespierre has gone little to Committee; but held himself apart, as if in a kind of pet. Nay they have made a Report on that old Catherine Theot, and her Regenerative Man spoken of by the Prophets; not in the best spirit. This Theot mystery they affect to regard as a Plot; but have evidently introduced a vein of satire, of irreverent banter, not against the Spinster alone, but obliquely against her Regenerative Man! Barrere's light pen was perhaps at the bottom of it: read through the solemn snuffling organs of old Vadier of the Surete Generale, the Theot Report had its effect; wrinkling the general Republican visage into an iron grin. Ought these things to be?

We note further that among the Prisoners in the Twelve Houses of Arrest, there is one whom we have seen before. Senhora Fontenai, born Cabarus, the fair Proserpine whom

183

Representative Tallien Pluto-like did gather at Bourdeaux, not without effect on himself! Tallien is home, by recall, long since, from Bourdeaux; and in the most alarming position. Vain that he sounded, louder even than ever, the note of Jacobinism, to hide past shortcomings: the Jacobins purged him out; two times has Robespierre growled at him words of omen from the Convention Tribune. And now his fair Cabarus, hit by denunciation, lies Arrested, Suspect, in spite of all he could do! – Shut in horrid pinfold of death, the Senhora smuggles out to her red-gloomy Tallien the most pressing entreaties and conjurings: Save me; save thyself. Seest thou not that thy own head is doomed; thou with a too fiery audacity; a Dantonist withal; against whom lie grudges? Are ye not all doomed, as in the Polyphemus Cavern; the fawningest slave of you will be but eaten last! – Tallien feels with a shudder that it is true. Tallien has had words of omen, Bourdon has had words, Freron is hated and Barras: each man 'feels his head if it yet stick on his shoulders.'

Meanwhile Robespierre, we still observe, goes little to Convention, not at all to Committee; speaks nothing except to his Jacobin House of Lords, amid his bodyguard of Tappe-durs. These 'forty-days,' for we are now far in July, he has not shewed face in Committee; could only work there by his three shallow scoundrels, and the terror there was of him. The Incorruptible himself sits apart; or is seen stalking in solitary places in the fields, with an intensely meditative air; some say, 'with eyes red-spotted,' (Deux Amis, xii. 347-73.) fruit of extreme bile: the lamentablest seagreen Chimera that walks the Earth that July! O hapless Chimera; for thou too hadst a life, and a heart of flesh, – what is this the stern gods, seeming to smile all the way, have led and let thee to!

Art not thou he who, few years ago, was a young Advocate of promise; and gave up the Arras Judgeship rather than sentence one man to die? –

What his thoughts might be? His plans for finishing the Terror? One knows not. Dim vestiges there flit of Agrarian Law; a victorious Sansculottism become Landed Proprietor; old Soldiers sitting in National Mansions, in Hospital Palaces of Chambord and Chantilly; peace bought by victory; breaches healed by Feast of Etre Supreme; – and so, through seas of blood, to Equality, Frugality, worksome Blessedness, Fraternity, and Republic of the virtues! Blessed shore, of such a sea of Aristocrat blood: but how to land on it? Through one last wave: blood of corrupt Sansculottists; traitorous or semi-traitorous Conventionals, rebellious Talliens, Billauds, to whom with my Etre Supreme I have become a bore; with my Apocalyptic Old Woman a laughing-stock! – So stalks he, this poor Robespierre, like a seagreen ghost through the blooming July. Vestiges of schemes flit dim. But what his schemes or his thoughts were will never be known to man.

New Catacombs, some say, are digging for a huge simultaneous butchery. Convention to be butchered, down to the right pitch, by General Henriot and Company: Jacobin House of Lords made dominant; and Robespierre Dictator. (Deux Amis, xii. 350-8.) There is actually, or else there is not actually, a List made out; which the Hairdresser has got eye on, as he frizzled the Incorruptible locks. Each man asks himself, Is it I?

Nay, as Tradition and rumour of Anecdote still convey it, there was a remarkable bachelor's dinner one hot day at Barrere's. For doubt not, O Reader, this Barrere and others of them gave dinners; had 'country-house at Clichy,' with elegant enough sumptuosities, and pleasures high-rouged! But at this dinner we speak of, the day being so hot, it is said, the guests all stript their coats, and left them in the drawing-room: whereupon Carnot glided out; groped in Robespierre's pocket; found a list of Forty, his own name among them; and tarried not at the wine-cup that day! – Ye must bestir yourselves, O Friends; ye dull Frogs of the Marsh, mute ever since Girondism sank under, even ye now must croak or die! Councils are held, with word and beck; nocturnal, mysterious as death. Does not a feline Maximilien stalk there; voiceless as yet; his green eyes red-spotted; back bent, and hair up? Rash Tallien, with his rash temper and audacity of tongue; he shall bell the cat. Fix a day; and be it soon, lest never!

Lo, before the fixed day, on the day which they call Eighth of Thermidor, 26th July 1794, Robespierre himself reappears in Convention; mounts to the Tribune! The biliary face seems clouded with new gloom; judge whether your Talliens, Bourdons listened with interest. It is a voice bodeful of death or of life. Long-winded, unmelodious as the screech-owl's, sounds that prophetic voice: Degenerate condition of Republican spirit; corrupt moderatism; Surete, Salut Committees themselves infected; back-sliding on this hand and on that; I, Maximilien, alone left incorruptible, ready to die at a moment's warning. For all which what remedy is there? The Guillotine; new vigour to the all-healing Guillotine: death to traitors of every hue! So sings the prophetic voice; into its Convention sounding-board. The old song this: but to-day, O Heavens! has the sounding-board ceased to act? There is not resonance in this Convention; there is, so to speak, a gasp of silence; nay a certain grating of one knows not what! – Lecointre, our old Draper of Versailles, in these questionable circumstances, sees nothing he can do so safe as rise, 'insidiously' or not insidiously, and move, according to established wont, that the Robespierre Speech be 'printed and sent to the Departments.' Hark: gratings, even of dissonance! Honourable Members hint dissonance; Committee-Members, inculpated in the Speech, utter dissonance; demand 'delay in printing.' Ever higher rises the note of dissonance; inquiry is even made by Editor Freron: "What has become of the Liberty of Opinions in this Convention?" The Order to print and transmit, which had got passed, is rescinded. Robespierre, greener than ever before, has to retire, foiled; discerning that it is mutiny, that evil is nigh.

GO DOWN TO.

Tallien's eyes beamed bright, on the morrow, Ninth of Thermidor 'about nine o'clock,' to see that the Convention had actually met. Paris is in rumour: but at least we are met, in Legal Convention here; we have not been snatched seriatim; treated with a Pride's Purge at the door. "Allons, brave men of the Plain," late Frogs of the Marsh! cried Tallien with a squeeze of the hand, as he passed in; Saint-Just's sonorous organ being now audible from the Tribune, and the game of games begun.

Saint-Just is verily reading that Report of his; green Vengeance, in the shape of Robespierre, watching nigh. Behold, however, Saint-Just has read but few sentences, when interruption rises, rapid crescendo; when Tallien starts to his feet, and Billaud, and this man starts and that, – and

Tallien, a second time, with his: "Citoyens, at the Jacobins last night, I trembled for the Republic. I said to myself, if the Convention dare not strike the Tyrant, then I myself dare; and with this I will do it, if need be," said he, whisking out a clear-gleaming Dagger, and brandishing it there: the Steel of Brutus, as we call it. Whereat we all bellow, and brandish, impetuous acclaim. "Tyranny; Dictatorship! Triumvirat!" And the Salut Committee-men accuse, and all men accuse, and uproar, and impetuously acclaim. And Saint-Just is standing motionless, pale of face; Couthon ejaculating, "Triumvir?" with a look at his paralytic legs. And Robespierre is struggling to speak, but President Thuriot is jingling the bell against him, but the Hall is sounding against him like an Aeolus-Hall: and Robespierre is mounting the Tribune-steps and descending again; going and coming, like to choke with rage, terror, desperation: – and mutiny is the order of the day!

O President Thuriot, thou that wert Elector Thuriot, and from the Bastille battlements sawest Saint-Antoine rising like the Ocean-tide, and hast seen much since, sawest thou ever the like of this? Jingle of bell, which thou jinglest against Robespierre, is hardly audible amid the Bedlam-storm; and men rage for life. "President of Assassins," shrieks Robespierre, "I demand speech of thee for the last time!" It cannot be had. "To you, O virtuous men of the Plain," cries he, finding audience one moment, "I appeal to you!" The virtuous men of the Plain sit silent as stones. And Thuriot's bell jingles, and the Hall sounds like Aeolus's Hall. Robespierre's frothing lips are grown 'blue;' his tongue dry, cleaving to the roof of his mouth. "The blood of Danton chokes him," cry they. "Accusation! Decree of Accusation!"

Thuriot swiftly puts that question. Accusation passes; the incorruptible Maximilien is decreed Accused.

Our fifth-act, of this natural Greek Drama, with its natural unities, can only be painted in gross; somewhat as that antique Painter, driven desperate, did the foam! For through this blessed July night, there is clangour, confusion very great, of marching troops; of Sections going this way, Sections going that; of Missionary Representatives reading Proclamations by torchlight; Missionary Legendre, who has raised force somewhere, emptying out the Jacobins, and flinging their key on the Convention table: "I have locked their door; it shall be Virtue that re-opens it." Paris, we say, is set against itself, rushing confused, as Ocean-currents do; a huge Mahlstrom, sounding there, under cloud of night. Convention sits permanent on this hand; Municipality most permanent on that. The poor Prisoners hear tocsin and rumour; strive to bethink them of the signals apparently of hope. Meek continual Twilight streaming up, which will be Dawn and a To-morrow, silvers the Northern hem of Night; it wends and wends there, that meek brightness, like a silent prophecy, along the great Ring-Dial of the Heaven. So still, eternal! And on Earth all is confused shadow and conflict; dissidence, tumultuous gloom and glare; and Destiny as yet shakes her doubtful urn.

About three in the morning, the dissident Armed-Forces have met. Henriot's Armed Force stood ranked in the Place de Greve; and now Barras's, which he has recruited, arrives there; and they front each other, cannon bristling against cannon. Citoyens! cries the voice of Discretion, loudly enough, Before coming to bloodshed, to endless civil-war, hear the Convention Decree read: 'Robespierre and all rebels Out of Law!' – Out of Law? There is terror in the sound: unarmed Citoyens disperse rapidly home; Municipal Cannoneers range themselves on the Convention side, with shouting. At which shout, Henriot descends from his upper room, far gone in drink as some say; finds his Place de Greve empty; the cannons' mouth turned towards him; and, on the whole, – that it is now the catastrophe!

Stumbling in again, the wretched drunk-sobered Henriot announces: "All is lost!" "Miserable! it is thou that hast lost it," cry they: and fling him, or else he flings himself, out of window: far enough down; into masonwork and horror of cesspool; not into death but worse. Augustin Robespierre follows him; with the like fate. Saint-Just called on Lebas to kill him: who would not. Couthon crept under a table; attempting to kill himself; not doing it. – On entering that Sanhedrim of Insurrection, we find all as good as extinct; undone, ready for seizure. Robespierre was sitting on a chair, with pistol shot blown through, not his head, but his under jaw; the suicidal hand had failed. Meda asserts that it was he who, with infinite courage, though in a lefthanded manner, shot Robespierre. Meda got promoted for his services of this night; and died General and Baron. Few credited Meda (in what was otherwise incredible.) With prompt zeal, not without trouble, we gather these wretched Conspirators; fish up even Henriot and Augustin, bleeding and foul; pack them all, rudely enough, into carts; and shall, before sunrise, have them safe under lock and key. Amid shoutings and embracings.

Robespierre lay in an anteroom of the Convention Hall, while his Prison-escort was getting ready; the mangled jaw bound up rudely with bloody linen: a spectacle to men. He lies stretched on a table, a deal-box his pillow; the sheath of the pistol is still clenched convulsively in his hand. Men bully him, insult him: his eyes still indicate intelligence; he speaks no word. 'He had on the sky-blue coat he had got made for the Feast of the Etre Supreme' – O reader, can thy hard heart hold out against that? His trousers were nankeen; the stockings had fallen down over the ankles. He spake no word more in this world.

And so, at six in the morning, a victorious Convention adjourns. Report flies over Paris as on golden wings; penetrates the Prisons; irradiates the faces of those that were ready to perish: turnkeys and moutons, fallen from their high estate, look mute and blue. It is the 28th day of July, called 10th of Thermidor, year 1794.

Fouquier had but to identify; his Prisoners being already Out of Law. At four in the afternoon, never before were the streets of Paris seen so crowded. From the Palais de Justice to the Place de la Revolution, for thither again go the Tumbrils this time, it is one dense stirring mass; all windows crammed; the very roofs and ridge-tiles budding forth human Curiosity, in strange gladness. The Death-tumbrils, with their motley Batch of Outlaws, some Twenty-three or so, from Maximilien to Mayor Fleuriot and Simon the Cordwainer, roll on. All eyes are on Robespierre's Tumbril, where he, his jaw bound in dirty linen, with his half-dead Brother, and half-dead Henriot, lie shattered; their 'seventeen hours' of agony about to end. The Gendarmes point their swords at him, to shew the people which is he. A woman springs on the Tumbril; clutching the side of it with one hand; waving the other Sibyl-like; and exclaims: "The death of thee gladdens my very heart, m'enivre de joie;" Robespierre opened his eyes; "Scelerat, go down to Hell, with the curses of all wives and mothers!" – At the foot of the scaffold, they stretched him on the ground till his turn came. Lifted aloft, his eyes again opened; caught the bloody axe. Samson wrenched the coat off him; wrenched the dirty linen from his jaw: the jaw fell powerless, there burst from him a cry; – hideous to hear and see. Samson, thou canst not be too quick!

Samson's work done, there burst forth shout on shout of applause. Shout, which prolongs itself not only over Paris, but over France, but over Europe, and down to this Generation. Deservedly, and also undeservedly. O unhappiest Advocate of Arras, wert thou worse than other Advocates? Stricter man, according to his Formula, to his Credo and his Cant, of probities, benevolences, pleasures-of-virtue, and such like, lived not in that age. A man fitted, in some luckier settled age, to have become one of those incorruptible barren Pattern-Figures, and have had marble-tablets and funeral-sermons! His poor landlord, the Cabinetmaker in the Rue Saint-Honore, loved him; his Brother died for him. May God be merciful to him, and to us.

This is end of the Reign of Terror; new glorious Revolution named of Thermidor; of Thermidor 9th, year 2; which being interpreted into old slave-style means 27th of July, 1794. Terror is ended; and death in the Place de la Revolution, were the 'Tail of Robespierre' once executed; which service Fouquier in large Batches is swiftly managing.

FINIS.

Homer's Epos, it is remarked, is like a Bas-relief sculpture: it does not conclude, but merely ceases. Such, indeed, is the Epos of Universal History itself. Directorates, Consulates, Emperorships, Restorations, Citizen-Kingships succeed this Business in due series, in due genesis one out of the other. Nevertheless the First-parent of all these may be said to have gone to air in the way we see. A Baboeuf Insurrection, next year, will die in the birth; stifled by the Soldiery. A Senate, if tinged with Royalism, can be purged by the Soldiery; and an Eighteenth of Fructidor transacted by the mere shew of bayonets. Nay Soldiers' bayonets can be used a posteriori on a Senate, and make it leap out of window, – still bloodless; and produce an Eighteenth of Brumaire. Such changes must happen: but they are managed by intriguings, caballings, and then by orderly word of command; almost like mere changes of Ministry. Not in general by sacred right of Insurrection, but by milder methods growing ever milder, shall the Events of French history be henceforth brought to pass.

It is admitted that this Directorate, which owned, at its starting, these three things, an 'old table, a sheet of paper, and an ink-bottle,' and no visible money or arrangement whatever, did wonders: that France, since the Reign of Terror hushed itself, has been a new France, awakened like a giant out of torpor; and has gone on, in the Internal Life of it, with continual progress. As for the External form and forms of Life, – what can we say except that out of the Eater there comes Strength; out of the Unwise there comes not Wisdom! Shams are burnt up; nay, what as yet is the peculiarity of France, the very Cant of them is burnt up. The new Realities are not yet come: ah no, only Phantasms, Paper models, tentative Prefigurements of such! In France there are now Four Million Landed Properties; that black portent of an Agrarian Law is as it were realised! What is still stranger, we understand all Frenchmen have 'the right of duel;' the Hackney-coachman with the Peer, if insult be given: such is the law of Public Opinion. Equality at least in death! The Form of Government is by Citizen King, frequently shot at, not yet shot.

On the whole, therefore, has it not been fulfilled what was prophesied, ex-postfacto indeed, by the Archquack Cagliostro, or another? He, as he looked in rapt vision and amazement into these things, thus spake: 'Ha! What is this? Angels, Uriel, Anachiel, and the other Five; Pentagon of Rejuvenescence; Power that destroyed Original Sin; Earth, Heaven, and thou Outer Limbo, which men name Hell! Does the EMPIRE OF IMPOSTURE waver? Burst there, in starry sheen updarting, Light-rays from out its dark foundations; as it rocks and heaves, not in travail-throes, but in death-throes? Yea, Light-rays, piercing, clear, that salute the Heavens, – lo, they kindle it; their starry clearness becomes as red Hellfire!

'IMPOSTURE is burnt up: one Red-sea of Fire, wild-billowing enwraps the World; with its fire-tongue, licks at the very Stars. Thrones are hurled into it, and Dubois mitres, and Prebendal Stalls that drop fatness, and – ha! what see I? – all the Gigs of Creation; all, all! Wo is me! Never since Pharaoh's Chariots, in the Red-sea of water, was there wreck of Wheel-vehicles like this in the Sea of Fire. Desolate, as ashes, as gases, shall they wander in the wind. Higher, higher yet flames the Fire-Sea; crackling with new dislocated timber;

hissing with leather and prunella. The metal Images are molten; the marble Images become mortar-lime; the stone Mountains sulkily explode. RESPECTABILITY, with all her collected Gigs inflamed for funeral pyre, wailing, leaves the earth: not to return save under new Avatar. Imposture, how it burns, through generations: how it is burnt up; for a time. The World is black ashes; which, ah, when will they grow green? The Images all run into amorphous Corinthian brass; all Dwellings of men destroyed; the very mountains peeled and riven, the valleys black and dead: it is an empty World! Wo to them that shall be born then! – A King, a Queen (ah me!) were hurled in; did rustle once; flew aloft, crackling, like paper-scroll. Iscariot Egalite was hurled in; thou grim De Launay, with thy grim Bastille; whole kindreds and peoples; five millions of mutually destroying Men. For it is the End of the Dominion of IMPOSTURE (which is Darkness and opaque Firedamp); and the burning up, with unquenchable fire, of all the Gigs that are in the Earth.' This Prophecy, we say, has it not been fulfilled, is it not fulfilling?

And so here, O Reader, has the time come for us two to part. Toilsome was our journeying together; not without offence; but it is done. To me thou wert as a beloved shade, the disembodied or not yet embodied spirit of a Brother. To thee I was but as a Voice. Yet was our relation a kind of sacred one; doubt not that! Whatsoever once sacred things become hollow jargons, yet while the Voice of Man speaks with Man, hast thou not there the living fountain out of which all sacrednesses sprang, and will yet spring? Man, by the nature of him, is definable as 'an incarnated Word.' Ill stands it with me if I have spoken falsely: thine also it was to hear truly. Farewell.